read your child's thoughts

read your child's thoughts

pre-school learning Piaget's way

Mary Sime

with 100 illustrations

Thames and Hudson

All photographs were taken by the author, except those on pages 12, 28 and 36 which were taken respectively by Mrs Hon Yin Holmes, Maurice Webster of 'Napcolour', Ormskirk, and Professor Brian Holmes

© 1980 Thames and Hudson Limited, London

Library of Congress Catalog card number 79–66138

Printed and bound in Great Britain by Jarrold and Sons Ltd, Norwich

CONTENTS

PREFACE

This book is intended chiefly for those parents who have the intellectual development of their pre-school child at heart. It holds out hope that they will enjoy finding time to play with him, to talk with him (from his first day of life onwards) and to enrich their own lives as well as his by watching his earliest gestures and explorations and, through them, interpreting his earliest thoughts.

A child of such parents is born with a gift as precious as the proverbial silver spoon in the mouth. However rich or poor his home is in material and financial terms, it is rich in the one thing he needs above all for a good start in life. This is the complete attention, at frequent if perhaps short intervals each and every day, of affectionate and genuinely interested people of whom instinctively he knows himself to be a part and who obviously respond to him as part of themselves. The fundamental psychological security that grows in him through sharing his babyhood and toddlerhood experiences with his mother (substantiated as far as possible by his father, his siblings and his grandparents) is as much a basic need as the physical security that most parents give unstintingly. There are innumerable books available to help a mother care for her child's physical needs, but few simple ones exist to help her study and nurture the growth of his intelligence in this period of intensive foundation-laying.

Today psychologists are constantly researching the mental development of the pre-school child and publishing their findings. One of the greatest of these research scholars, Professor Jean Piaget of Geneva, has earned world-wide fame during the past half-century for his discoveries about the biological basis of a child's intellectual growth. Piaget started his career as a biologist and has combined his biology with developmental psychology to become perhaps the greatest epistemologist of all time.

Piaget's books are numerous, scholarly and difficult to read in English translations, but his thesis is simple. It is that a human being absorbs learning through interaction with his environment.

Piaget, in his books and learned papers, describes in detail how he and his research teams set out scientifically to monitor this learning process. In this book and in its companion volume, *A Child's Eye View*, an attempt has been made to give an outline of Piaget's methods and results. This book deals with pre-school days and the other follows through to early adult life. The two books inevitably have some overlap, just as the first and second sections of this book must overlap.

As many as possible of the Piagetian diagnostic tests have been made in non-clinical conditions with English children and have been recorded here verbally and photographically. Many tests are as simple as merely offering a baby a toy to clutch. Others need no administering but simply demand observation, in the way that Piaget observed and recorded within his own family circle. Where diagnostic tests *are* administered children love them, not realizing that they are anything more serious than play or puzzles. So it could be hoped that parents might find it inspiring to record, in diary form, both photographically and in words, each milestone in the learning process as their own child reaches it.

Some parents, with guidance from this book, might not want to go further than such observation and recording. Most, however, would want to diagnose from the results how to enrich the child's environment with increasing challenges so as to intensify his learning process.

Students of developmental psychology who are working towards qualifications will find here a fairly complete outline of the subtle changes of behaviour, easy to monitor in the baby and toddler, that denote growth from one intellectual period to the next. As a final section to each chapter there are paragraphs aimed at the more serious student, which give Piaget's technical terms for what has been written in simpler English in the main part of the chapter. In these paragraphs there are also slightly more scientific explanations. Parents, of course, may wish to keep pace with this 'heavier' reading too, but those who want to read only the simpler part of each chapter should still get the full story.

Although *Read your Child's Thoughts* is based *primarily* on the researches of Piaget into the patterns of thinking that a very young child builds up in a happy and alert family setting, references have been made slightly beyond Piaget's theories. The book stretches to interpretations of Piaget's findings, as contrasted to simply reporting them, especially where more recent research than his on a particular theme seems to substantiate his results.

I would appeal to parents and students who read this book only, without the companion one, to realize that it by no means covers the full breadth and depth of Piaget's work. Nor does it give a sense of the intensity of his research. Yet it picks out faithfully the general pattern of early intellectual development and attempts to simplify it enough to make it enjoyable.

This enjoyable reading should not mean reading straight through. It is not a book to read at a sitting nor to read within a week as one might read a novel. It is to keep beside you for reference, as you keep your cookery or gardening book. It is for you to read a chapter at a time, month by month or year by year as your child grows up. In this way, as you study what lies behind your child's mental growth, and marvel at it, you will be inspired to respond to his needs both conversationally and through increasing the subjects for exploration in his environment. You can do this, without over-stimulating or harassing him, from the first day of his life until *after* the time that he may possibly have overtaken you in intellectual prowess. Such fundamentally secure learning is a basis for a balanced personality in later life.

My gratitude is due to many people for their help.

I would begin with 'Small', alias Andrew, who for nearly two years acted as chief 'guinea pig' for my students and me, and to his mother, Mrs Anne Brownlow, who not only brought him to college regularly but also joined in the fun. I think it may have been 'Small' who triggered off this book.

This leads me on to thank *all* the many parents who have either joined in or stood by with great patience while I administered diagnostic tests, or waited, almost interminably, for a child to repeat a psychologically illustrative movement that I needed to photograph. Other parents have waited for weeks for their child to show particular symptoms of the dawning of a new intellectual stage and have then telephoned, inviting me to go to their homes to record and to photograph. It would be almost superfluous to thank their children: they (except for Janet in her bath) enjoyed the processes beyond needing further reward.

I must also thank a friend, Margery Pollard, for taking on the task of typing the manuscript of the book in such a cheerful and efficient manner.

I would thank Maurice Webster, a manager of 'Napcolour' in Ormskirk, for the personal supervision he gave to the processing of my photographs. Many areas within photographs had to be enlarged with great skill and exactness to emphasize specific psychological points, and his patience never waned.

I also thank Mrs Islip, headmistress of the County Nursery School at Chorley, and Mr Brodie, headmaster of Essex County Primary School at Tollesbury, for their helpfulness in letting me (and in the former case my students) test and photograph children under their care.

As I always end by saying, most gratitude of all is due to Piaget himself. To his books and papers I owe the substance that is the backbone of this book and that has been an enriching influence on my career.

MARY SIME,
Tollesbury, Essex,
16 March 1979

GENERAL INTRODUCTION

As research increases, we come to realize ever more clearly the extreme value to a child of parent-based early education. This in itself brings a need for the parents to study the developmental psychology of early childhood so that they can nurture the growth of their child's first mental patterns. Any parent who has the will to do this finds it a sure way of helping the baby himself to lay firm foundations for his own future intellectual ability and for the psychological steadiness of character that will result from it. But this is not just suggested extra work for busy parents. It is suggested extra pleasure, too. Parents can find great happiness and interest in penetrating their child's early thoughts: this happiness will also infect the child, in turn enhancing the scope of his more intense learning.

In later years such parent-based early education is bound to pay dividends, for the child will become confident rather than precocious. Early complete mother-dependence is natural in the child and even in babyhood he extends it, to a lesser degree, to other members of his immediate family. Nevertheless, dependence on the mother remains paramount. If this is satisfied the child becomes selectively trustful. During late toddlerhood there is no hazard in gently encouraging any child who has laid such secure foundations to socialize with a few others of his age, and he will do so happily and without sudden shock. Gentleness is the keynote: widening of his horizons could shatter all the earlier good work unless it is carried out first *within* the security of his mother's presence or proximity and then, still gradually, without her near him for only very short periods of time. By the time he enters school at the age of five the roots of learning that mother-care has planted in him will be secure and strong and he will be ready for the longer hours of socialization with his peers that are typical of first school life.

Piaget's general theme of intellectual development rests on the child's mental maturation being geared to his interaction with his environment, for there is a natural urge in every human being to learn in this way. One can see it start from the day of birth: those of you reading this book still learn by such interaction and will continue to do so well into old age. The challenges that his environment offers to each particular child can be enhanced by an alert parent adapting and enriching that environment with appropriate toys and responses as she monitors the child's particular interests and needs. Such a parent is, in fact, the richest element in the environment. The other people in a close-knit family play an almost equal role.

THE FIVE MAIN PERIODS OF INTELLECTUAL GROWTH

Except for people of limited ability, every young person passes through five major periods of intellectual growth. Each of us reaches these five periods in the same sequence but at different rates, dictated not only by innate ability but also by the varied stimulation that we meet on the way. In each period each of us builds for himself learning processes and mental as well as physical skills characteristic of the period. These skills are never lost. They accumulate as we mature from each period to the next, acting as the foundations from which the mental skills of the next period evolve.

Readers who understand this book will have reached the last such period. You probably reached it during adolescence. Such readers can think abstractly and, if need be, can solve problems completely in their heads. Because of that ability you think differently from much younger people and perhaps you become impatient and try verbally to persuade them to think in your way. By such verbal persuasion and reasoning you may manage to influence adolescents, because most of them are feeling their way into this fifth period too, but pre-adolescents, except for the very gifted, simply *cannot* see your point of view. They have not the mental tools with which to do so. Similarly, you find it difficult and perhaps impossible to think as they do because you cannot prevent your nimble thoughts from leaping ahead. You *cannot* limit your thinking to their way of thinking but you *can*, nevertheless, watch and understand how they think and adapt your persuading powers to their mental abilities.

There are, of course, a very few extremely gifted children who speed through to adult achievements, seeming to telescope childhood. But for almost all of us the five major periods of intellectual growth are as follows:

1 Babyhood:

During this period (of which we shall look at the six sub-periods in the first six chapters) learning is predominantly dependent on experience that a child gains through constant close proximity to his mother and through the child's own senses of touch, taste, smell, sight and hearing. As he moves his arms, legs, head and mouth, by inherited reflex actions, he absorbs into himself the essence of what his senses tell him. Thus, as we see in the example of Marieke, learning begins. And thus, from the beginning and for the rest of his life, the child's learning will be not only within the brain but throughout the whole biology of his nervous system. Patterns of such learning build up during babyhood and lay foundations for the intellectual growth that accrues, at an ever-increasing rate, as further periods are reached and passed through.

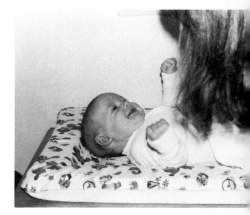

Marieke. Egocentric communication.

Ruth forming early preconcepts.

2 Toddlerhood:

This is a period during which, with the onset of greater physical mobility and the fairly rapid growth of language, the child builds up ideas and notions (which psychologists call 'preconcepts') about the things and activities that he enjoys. He builds in his mind what Piaget calls an interior 'model'[1] of his world made up of patterns that are shaky and ephemeral generalizations. These patterns are not only mental visual pictures: they involve records of sounds, feelings, tastes and smells and they have the power to motivate him to further exploration. The child finds ways of talking about them either by gestures or by developing speech. Ruth, in the accompanying picture, is doing all these things. Speech, in its turn, helps him to substantiate the learning process. He communicates his thoughts about these dynamic pictures inside himself *to* himself as well as to adults, through his play and his imitation and art.

The period is known by most psychologists as one of 'parallel play'. If the toddler is put among other children for too long he will play in a lonely way *among* them rather than *with* them, enjoying the wealth of toys and only *seeming* to play with the children and to enjoy their companionship. Yet with his parents play is sociable and packed with happy, undisturbed learning.

3 The Intuitive Period:

This is Piaget's own term for a period for which various parts of the English-speaking world have different names. Americans refer to youngsters in this period as 'preschoolers and first-graders'. The British call them 'infants'. The Australian speaks delightfully of 'the kindy child'. In all cases they are speaking of children who are, without adult persuasion, beginning to play with other children in a social way.

In the first place, play in the intuitive period tends to be with one (ephemeral) favourite friend. This subtle difference from the parallel play of the previous period is important. It indicates that the child is now intellectually ready to share ideas rather than just to share toys with others of his age. This, in its turn, indicates a readiness to begin to appreciate the intangible and to handle, intuitively only, abstract ideas such as those of number or sequence. Between the ages of about five and seven such a child, through constant intuitive response to (for example) number situations, will become deeply interested in them in a preconceptual way and will finally form a number concept. During the span of this period he should form concepts of area, sequence and length too, by a slow process that he finds laborious but enjoyable. In the picture we see a class of six-year-olds from an English village infants' school (Tollesbury in Essex) developing such concepts through organized play.

A mother must not jump too easily to conclusions that her child *has* formed these, or other simple concepts, merely because she sees early signs of their dawning. For example, an ability to count is not a concept of number; it is just one early milestone on the route to it.

The very young forming earliest concepts.

---

[1] The word 'model' is used in its mathematical, dynamic sense.

4 Junior days:

Juniors, Nicholas and Michael, reasoning concretely.

From the age of about seven or eight onwards a child can become almost defiantly self-reliant and self-assured. He also becomes very sociable within small gangs of his chosen friends. During the intuitive period his rapidly maturing mental structure gradually gave him the sense of security that enabled him to turn away naturally, for gradually lengthening periods, from dependence on his parents and other trusted adults. Now comes an equally healthy desire to shake off too much adult supervision and to play, and to work at learning, in small friendship groups of his peers. Boys and girls tend to separate into groups of their own sex. It is a period of 'ganging up' constructively, generally with no destructive intentions. Within such groups there is a strong bond of friendship and of trust and respect. With true group-mentality juniors feel an urge to create things and to enjoy their environment, for example to build a tree-house or to clear rubbish for a small football pitch – perhaps even to plant a garden. They feel a real hankering, as a team, to overcome any problems that may arise. Consequently reasoning becomes their dominant mental activity. Such reasoning is aided by the newly formed concepts that now dynamically press to be exercised. But, throughout junior life, these concepts are too insecure to function in isolation. There is a need in each child to share the equally insecure conceptual thoughts of his peers and to steady his thoughts by working them out on material things. We see Nicholas and Michael (aged ten and eight years) who had been exploring the property of a lens for turning light into heat. Michael tries to teach his toddler brother Neil to set fire to a shaving of wood by this method.

13

Jane. The onset of hypothetical thought.

Comparative diagram of early schooling patterns.

5 Adolescence:

This is the period of the richest mental development of all for any young person, not only in building up a reasonable fund of factual knowledge but above all in building skills of elegant language and patterns of reasoning. He will now gradually slip into reasoning that does not need the help of materials to steady his thoughts. We see the dawn of hypothetical thinking in the pensive gaze of Jane. As glandular development tends to stimulate unrest in the adolescent, his confident ability to think calmly should come to his rescue and help him to take sensible and happy paths towards becoming a contributing member of society; if, on the contrary, his foundations of thought have been laid insecurely in earlier days, it is during adolescence that turbulence may erupt. The first alternative is what most fair-minded parents want for their growing children. The help that loving parents give their children before schooling and during their early schooling could be the root of stable character. And the ability to give this help depends on parental understanding of the child's patterns of thinking as much as on understanding either his physical growth or the subject-matter that he is to learn.

FOR THE MORE SERIOUS STUDENT

The five periods of intellectual growth are known professionally as:

1 The Sensory-Motor Period, because of the use of the senses motivating the child, through reflex movements of the limbs, etc., to explore and interact with his immediate environment and to learn through this interaction.

2 The Preconceptual Period, because of the growth of preconcepts which will be dealt with in some detail in the second section of this book.

3 The Intuitive Period, for now the child uses preconcepts as the basis of illogical and intuitive reasoning. During this period many elementary concepts are formed.

4 The Concrete Operational Period, because the child's thinking operates and reasons within the steadying effect of dependence on concrete things.

5 The Period of Abstract Thinking, or *of Hypothetical Reasoning*.

Students will have noticed that periods 3, 4 and 5 coincide approximately with the predominant pattern of school transfers in Britain, most of the United States and parts of Australia such as New South Wales. Other areas, such as South Australia, differ only slightly but still coincide. This pattern should enable teachers to specialize in teaching methods suitable to the intellectual ability of pupils in the period concerned. If the teachers can do this with psychological wisdom it should have an obvious value. A few local authority areas in Britain are trying instead to achieve a less obvious but equally valuable result. They

Age	USA	England (General System)	England (Alternative System)	Australia (South Australia)	Australia (New South Wales)	Piaget's Periods (approximate)
4+	Kindergarten (voluntary)	Nursery school or play school (voluntary)		Pre-school or kindergarten (voluntary)	Pre-school (Voluntary)	Preconceptual
5+		Infants' school	First school	Prep class	Kindergarten	Intuitive
6+	Grade 1			Year 1	Class 1	
7+	Grade 2	Junior school		Year 2	Class 2	
8+	Grade 3			Year 3	Class 3	Concrete operational
9+	Grade 4		Middle school	Year 4	Class 4	
10+	Grade 5			Year 5	Class 5	
11+	Grade 6	Secondary school		Year 6	Class 6	
12+	Grade 7			Year 7	Class 7	Intermittent formal thinking
13+	Grade 8			Year 8	Class 8	
14+				Year 9	Class 9	

are beginning to apply the old public school pattern of transferring at the ages of about eight or nine and thirteen or fourteen. Thus children in what are known as 'middle schools' need teachers skilled in two different ways of serving their intellectual needs, who can support each child in his possible mental turmoil as he grows from one way of thinking to the next. The diagram accompanying will clarify these points.

The advanced student should keep it clear in his mind that, in Piagetian theory, learning is not just memories in the brain together with skills such as speech and reasoning patterns. It is an integrating and maturing of the complete human being, controlled by the brain, into a complicated person who is both intellectually and physically mature. Piaget would say that 'it has a biologically and epistemological dimension'. Study of this process now goes under the name of 'epistemology', which is the science of studying intelligence.

Introduction to Section I
Babyhood

The egocentricity of babyhood, mentioned in the general introduction, which causes a baby to show his utter dependence on adult help and to make uninhibited demands for it, is paralleled by his quick response to adult affection. Of course this response is not gratitude, for the egocentrism in him cannot recognize altruism in others. It is an acceptance so total as to be a complete surrender of himself to the adult's ministrations and so to the adult as a person. Egocentricity, which we tend to reject when we see it in adults, is half the charm of babyhood.

Egocentricity is at first so complete that the baby feels himself to be part of his mother, to rest assured that she feels his hunger or his discomfort and, as the weeks and months go by, that she feels his need for a toy or a game. Of course he cannot at first think these things but can only 'rest assured'. As he begins to think clearly he takes it for granted that she thinks his thoughts with him. It is sometimes said that just as an adult thinks socially, even when alone, so a small child thinks egocentrically even when in company.

Whatever a child of egocentric age demands he really needs (unless, of course, an adult can recognize hidden danger in it), because such a child cannot imagine privileges, nor can he think of the unnecessary. Similarly, and consequently, he has no power to be grateful since, by egocentricity, everything around him seems to be part of him and consequently his by right. The sense of security given to him during this period by a parent who responds generously and patiently to his demands for attention lays a foundation of mental security to last the rest of the child's life. He cannot afford to have his nascent thoughts cluttered by fears or frustrations. The long period of egocentricity (followed by a further long one of semi-egocentricity and parental dependence, to be studied in Section II) is probably the greatest reason for man's brain having developed so much more than the brain of any other animal.

And so, for a mother and soon for a father too, ministering to a baby's needs means much more than providing physical necessities. Food, comfort, shelter, warmth are supplied by most animals to their young. In contrast there are parts of the world where, because of over-population or refugee conditions, human babies do *not* have their physical needs satisfied. Yet even in those most materially deprived communities one finds mothers instinctively trying to give babies more than physical care. Such active and sustained mother-companionship is of inestimable value to them. It lays in such children foundations for mental alertness, thus preparing them to fend sensibly for themselves in the difficult situations that must lie ahead.

In the richness of the Western world a child can be doubly fortunate. In the first place he can be directly so because of material richness. But he can also be indirectly fortunate because material security frees his mother to lavish her time and attention upon him, to divine his thoughts and so to build a happy and balanced mind in a healthy body.

Babyhood is a major period in a child's intellectual life. A parent who wishes to study her child's development in that period can most easily do so by breaking it down into six sub-periods.

The accumulation of methods of learning is so rapid over the eighteen months or two years that sub-periods can be clearly defined.

THE SIX INTELLECTUAL SUB-PERIODS WITHIN BABYHOOD[1]

Sub-period 1 covers about the first month of life during which, through reflex actions that are triggered off by needs, a baby learns to grope accurately for the food that is offered to him and to appeal for attention and affection. Sometimes his successes are greater than at other times and he gradually becomes able to distinguish enjoyable results from unpleasant ones. He gazes reflexively towards anything that disturbs one of his senses. Hal, at ten days old, reflexively grasped his mother's thumb while paying alert attention to the snapping sound of his sister's toy.[*]

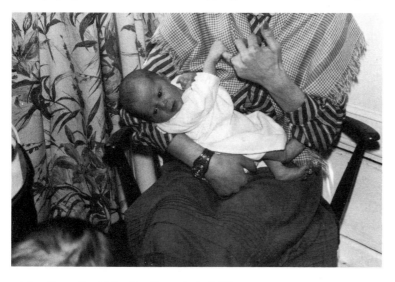

Hal, sub-period 1. Reflex response to a snapping sound.

[1] Jean Piaget, *The Origin of Intelligence in the Child.*

[*] These photographs will be referred to in Chapters Two to Six.

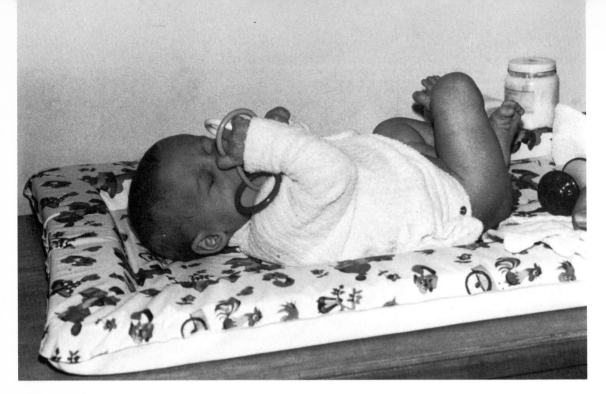

Marieke, sub-period 2. Simple
reflexive clutching.

Marieke, sub-period 3. Aiming at
specific results.

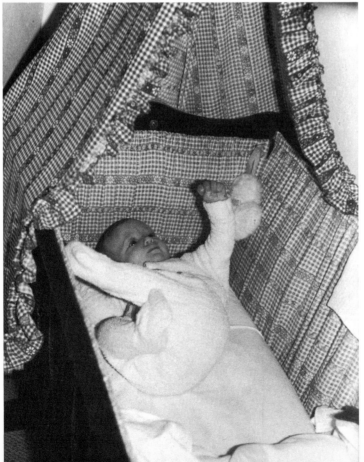

'Small', sub-period 4. Exploring with his
gums.

Sub-period 2: It is roughly in his second and third months that a baby first seems to take a real interest in his own activities. He starts to extend those activities beyond serving basic survival needs. He starts pursuing results for their own sake. We see Marieke struggling with hands and feet alike to clutch a string of plastic toys for pleasure.*

Sub-period 3: In about the fourth month his activities become far less random. They are centred on results. Again we see Marieke, this time trying to influence a toy that is swinging in her cot roof.*

Sub-period 4: Now comes a sub-period in which the baby will not form any new patterns of learning but will link together and consolidate past achievements. He will practise activities that are patterns of exploration centred on results and will search for new materials and new situations in which to perfect and interlink his existing habits. 'Small', exploring a ring of keys by sucking them, illustrates this.*

Sub-period 5: By the time the baby is about ten months old a long sub-period of active experimentation begins, generally with a particular interest in processes and a desire for novelty. Mark has recently discovered the novelty of building a tower and then enjoying the feeling of bricks cascading all around him as he kicks it down again.*

Sub-period 6: By the age of about eighteen or twenty months a baby's transition into toddlerhood begins. He experiments with linking his existing skills. Now he begins to coordinate situations *in his mind* enough to have flashes of insight. When Paul James's tractor broke down he had the insight to search for a hole to be mended. He tried one screwdriver in the hole, then two together. He struggled in this way for half an hour although the hole was completely unrelated to the breakdown.*

As the sixth sub-period ends, the child will pass from babyhood to the intellectual level of a toddler and a talkative little person.

Mark, sub-period 5. An elementary experiment.

Paul James, sub-period 6. Foresight in an experiment.

19

FOR THE MORE SERIOUS STUDENT
BABYHOOD, THE SENSORY-MOTOR PERIOD

In the six sub-periods of the Sensory-Motor Period the patterns of mental activity and understanding that the child forms are known technically as 'schemas' or 'schemata'. The activities that are used in building up these schemata are assimilation and accommodation. They will be enlarged upon in Chapter One.

In each of the next six chapters we monitor a child's way of assimilating and accommodating as he explores and interacts with his environment. We must remember that his environment is not just a world of inanimate and still things. It is a world of activities and, above all, of people who can help him to enrich his life, directly by mere companionship and indirectly by sharing his growing interests. This offers him the maximum chance of learning through his own experiences.

Professor Luria's recent research goes a long way towards proving that a brain that is constantly exercised actually grows in weight, and that the average size of the human brain has shown steady increase within historical time. This increase could well be the result of parents being able to give greater attention to their children as economic security has emerged.

The main thing to stress is that intellectual growth in babyhood is quite as rapid as physical growth. Both aspects of growth have maximum chances of success if the child is serene and contented in his mother's constant presence. To help him in his learning we need to watch not only *what* he is learning but also *how* he is learning. We can share his thoughts with him. Then we can encourage him and enjoy caring for him.

Some psychologists claim that the constant mother-care lavished upon children brought up in the bleakest of refugee camps can account for their generally high intellectual ability as they grow up. It is their only luxury but it is in plentiful supply because the parents' restricted movement frees all their time for them to give to their children.

CHAPTER ONE

Babyhood, Period 1[1]
A Bundle of Reflexes,
Programmed for Learning

A baby arrives in the world programmed to grope for food and to suck, to sneeze, to wave his arms and legs, and to grasp with his hands anything that touches the palms. He will grasp with his feet too, but less well. He will gaze with vague eyes, but will not at first follow any moving point of light or dim figure revealed by that light. Figures and light alike are vague and without form, and they merge shapelessly into the background.

REFLEX ACTIONS

All the baby's reflex actions have survival value. A sneeze, purely a reflex in itself, clears his nostrils. His reflexive grasp of what touches the palm of his hands is soon strong enough, if need be, to take his own weight. Then there are other reflexes that have not only an immediate and direct survival value, but also a more subtle one in channelling messages to his brain and initiating a process of learning that will ensure safety for him in his life as a whole. Such obvious reflexes as movements of his head, neck and mouth, of his flailing arms and stretching legs, bring him into contact with the features of his small environment. Some of the resulting experiences are enjoyable to his touch; others are not. He feels the soft warmth of his mother and it sends a message of pleasure to his brain; other tactile experiences tell of discomfort and set off loud cries. Similarly, any relevant element in his environment will trigger into activity a reflex action appropriate to the sense concerned. For about the first month of his life he will be utterly dependent upon these involuntary reflexes for making contact with and exploring his own small world of people and things around him.

Janet Claire illustrates many of these points. She was a peaceful and contented baby. She had been born into a dimly lit room and within ten minutes or so had started gazing towards the light from two distant windows. She quickly learned to feed effectively. Nothing worried her except her bath.

[1] This chapter is based on Jean Piaget, *The Origin of Intelligence*, Chapter 1.

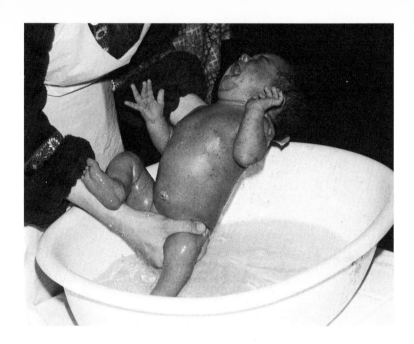

Janet Claire. Defensive reflexes in action.

Janet Claire. Reflexive clutching.

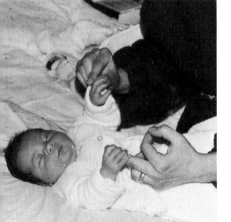

At six days old she was photographed, screaming at the feeling of insecurity that bathing brought to her. Every muscle in her body became tense and sprang into defensive activity. She flailed her arms in an effort to grasp support and pressed her feet hard on the end of the basin. As she was lifted out her right foot tried to lock on to a sleeve of her mother's dress that touched it by chance. She quietened and relaxed as she was dried and dressed. Then came the drowsiness that precedes sleep. She fell asleep gently clutching her mother's finger in quiet contentment.

Janet Claire learned fast. Within another week she was actively enjoying her bath and the gentle talk (and the occasional music) that accompanied it.

The exercising of these survival reflexes, even in this first month of life, starts the baby on a road of discovery and conquest of everything close to him, if sufficient scope is given to him to interact freely. Nathan Isaacs speaks of the child as 'architect of his own growth':[2] in so far as that means his mental growth, he is in fact such an architect and builder too.

But this is leaping ahead too fast. In the child's first few days most of his activities are completely random except in the sense that some internal clock regulates sensations such as hunger and a need to sleep. It is chance which governs what things touch his hand to make him clutch, or what objects catch the attention of his eyes and ears. In the first day or so, many a baby may take time exploring to find a nipple; and after initial help from his mother, and early successes, he may again equally well start by exploring in the wrong direction. The reflex causes him to continue to explore. The reward of success has a modifying effect on later attempts, for right paths are somehow registered in his nervous system. So,

[2] Nathan Isaacs, *The Growth of Understanding in the Young Child.*

22

gradually, he learns. At each succeeding meal his reflex actions take on a neater and more controlled course, and he builds a scheme of satisfactory action into his whole mechanism.

Even when the very young baby is still and drowsy his reflexes will spring quickly into action and waken him if one of his senses is disturbed. We read of Piaget's one-day-old son[3] being roused by a cry of other children and crying too. On his fourth day, after further such experiences, he cried loudly even when it was his father who made a gentle whimpering sound. Was such learning, we wonder, directly due to reflex crying being triggered off each time by the chance hearing of such a sound or was it due to the cuddling that probably always followed it? In all probability it was due to a combination of the two, for the essence of both must have been absorbed into his growing mental patterns.

Improvements in these, as in other schemes of activity that the baby develops in the first four or five weeks, may be slow or fast. Speed matters little so long as improvements are sure. In this way he will form his first habits. Then we shall see habits of efficiency, saving him time and energy, that will be diverted to other enjoyments as he enters the second period of babyhood at about a month old.

EGOCENTRICITY

Some part of the tiny baby's reflexes is likely to be in a state of constant activity whenever he is fully awake. If his arms and feet are unencumbered with clothing, they will be activated by the slightest touch. Perhaps his hand will clutch a finger that touches it, and even if at that moment he is crying he will be likely to stop instantly and show interest in the achievement. One cannot tell for sure whether or not the interest is more in the finger that the baby clutches than in the comfort of the clutching action itself. Whichever it is, something of the feel and texture will be assimilated into the mental patterns that he is building. But one thing will be certain: he will have no idea whether what he holds is or is not part of himself.

It seems that the baby's satisfaction is more often with the enriching feeling, almost as of success, produced by his own actions than with the object that precipitates the reflex. Why otherwise should he absorb enough learning to improve in actions that produce no other reward? Sometimes he may even seem to grasp at a sound and be contented by it.

Before her bath (see p. 22) Janet Claire was lying on her side. She flung her arm forward reflexively so that by chance it pointed to a toy, well beyond her reach. Her eyes, unable to focus, gazed at it and her hand pointed and then closed in an empty, grasping action which seemed to satisfy her. The toy was moved to just within her reach: still gazing at it she flung her arm, with pointing finger, so that she just brushed the toy, then contentedly she relaxed. For her the toy had no substance nor permanent existence, but the activity it precipitated had given her pleasure and learning.

[3] Jean Piaget, *Play, Dreams and Imitation in Childhood*, p. 7.

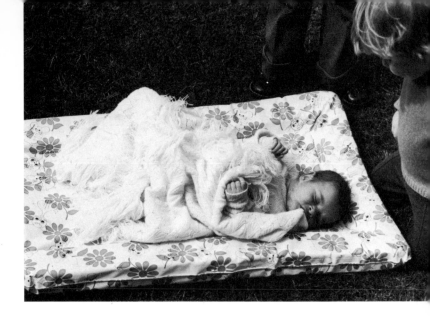

Christine. Near-discrimination.

DISCRIMINATION

Three-week-old Christine had cried for food for several minutes before this photograph was taken. Several times her brothers tried to staunch the crying by giving her her shawl to suck. She sucked each time for a few minutes before accommodating to the situation and turning her head away. When she was picked up she tried to suck my sleeve, then turned away from that in the same way. Her power of discriminating was dawning but was still slow to act.

After a further week or two, this power of discrimination will develop into knowing which things feel as if they should be avoided, which should be sucked to enjoy the feeling of sucking, which should be sucked and swallowed. Such discrimination will, of course, come earlier or later depending on external circumstances. For it must be remembered that throughout this first period of babyhood all activities will be reflexes triggered off by chance happenings of the moment and everything will seem to the child to be indistinguishable from himself.

HIS MOTHER, A SPECIAL CASE

Predominant among the causes of reflex actions will be hunger for food and for human companionship. This hunger for companionship is, of all needs, the easiest for a mother to ignore. Yet it is just as vital a need as any other if the child is to grow into a peaceful and sociable human being. His mother is the single most important element in his environment. From the beginning, while still feeling her to be part of himself, he distinguishes her from any other person.

So important is she to him that, well before the end of the first month, he forms a pattern of reaction to her that will become more generally applied only in the next period of babyhood. By the time he is three or four weeks old he may not only have learned to distinguish her voice from any other but he will turn his head seemingly to try to see her voice. If she responds by approaching and talking to him his own response will be vigorous and energetic.

Amber's response, towards the end of this first period, was typical.

As her mother talked to her, Amber waved a wide-arm welcome in rhythm with her mother's speech. She made facial gestures and gestures with her mouth that seemed to be imitations of her mother's, yet they could not be imitations, for not only had Amber never seen her own face but also her focus on her mother's must still have been blurred. Only the habit Amber had already formed of exercising reflexes the more enthusiastically in her mother's presence could account for the fact that these particular reflexes in her repertoire had become so controlled.

Her mother's frequent gentle talk had gradually roused in her the reflexes that stimulate the mouth and tongue muscles to attempt speech; yet her throat muscles strove unsuccessfully to control her voice and Amber only achieved the blowing of an occasional tiny bubble. On this occasion it was Amber who had set up the attempted conversation and her delighted mother who imitated her.

And so the month-old baby will have learned above all that he himself, by his own personality, can cause his mother to react not only to his needs but, if he is fortunate, to react also to his earliest interest. Yet he cannot realize that she does not feel exactly the same urge as he feels, for his egocentricity makes mother and child part of one another. He cannot, in fact, *think*. Learning comes before thinking. It is the sensuous experience that he shares with his mother.

It is equally important to both the mother and the baby that she should study and join in with his earliest learning in this way. She will find pleasure and enrichment in watching and understanding his learning techniques: he, by something akin to contagion, will feel her joy as well as his own. She will learn enough to be stimulated to supply him with appropriate, often costless, playthings that will give him even more exciting sensuous experiences to learn from. Above all, she will increasingly enjoy the habit of giving him her time and attention for purely social satisfaction.

So, as he passes to his second period of babyhood, he will have laid for himself the foundation of his future intellectual growth, in a month of interaction with an environment of which his mother is the chief feature. Other members of the family will have featured in it, too, and become recognizable. He will have grown to accept them as enjoyable elements in it although it will still not be clear to him that they (like his cot and his pram and his toys) are anything other than parts of himself. Above all his mother will continue to seem to be a vital part of his own being, exuding physical and mental security.

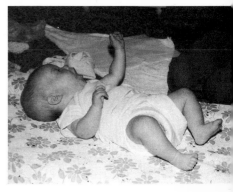

Amber. Earliest speech efforts.

FOR THE MORE SERIOUS STUDENT
SENSORY-MOTOR PERIOD, SUB-PERIOD 1,
SURVIVAL REFLEXES

A In reading Piaget's own accounts of his researches into this first sub-period of the sensory-motor period the student will find the following technical terms:

1 Assimilation: The process of absorbing the essence of an experience into the mind and into the whole bodily structure. In this sub-period assimilation is always through reflex actions but in later sub-periods (while reflexes will still play their part) it will also be through all learning techniques to date, as they accumulate. Assimilation is basic to life.

2 Schemas or *schemata* or *schemes:* The internal models (in the dynamic mathematical sense) of learning which are formed from assimilation, and which are later modified by accommodation, become patterns of mental and physical behaviour.

3 Accommodation: The adjustment of schemas, or of a specific action, to a special unusualness in the known environment. Accommodation therefore leads to 'progressive assimilation' of the essence of the new experience. Piaget calls this act of distinguishing 'recognitory assimilation'.

4 Motor recognition: This is the child's first active organization: for example, sucking to feed (if hungry), to play (see next period) and to comfort himself (e.g. thumb-sucking) all have different meanings for the child.

B Piaget acknowledges the theory of Claparède (*L'Education Fonctionelle*) that useful acts reproduce themselves for the simple reason that they answer a need. But Piaget, through his science of epistemology, goes further to show two things:
(i) *how* they answer the need, and
(ii) that the need is part of the process and not just a cause of it. It is all part of the endless circular or spiral process of learning that we shall study in the next five chapters.

C It is essential to realize that the reflexes of the first months of babyhood are not isolated actions. Each reflex involves the whole baby – body and brain. Janet Claire demonstrated this (p. 22). Each reflex is triggered off by a chance stimulus (which may be a basic need, such as hunger, or may be quite fortuitous) and then the whole child responds with rhythmic *integrated* movements. So schemas are registered in the mind and in the whole nervous system. They can be reactivated by a repetition of any part of themselves.

D A 'basic need' is not the same thing as a 'want' although to a mother watching her baby in the first or second sub-periods it can seem to be the same. For instance, he *needs* food. He can *seem to want* a toy that his hand has pointed to by chance (in or out of reach) and that his eyes have then focused upon. If he does clutch it he enjoys and registers the result but he has not wanted it for he cannot yet know that it exists in its own, isolated state. And, except obliquely, he does not need it.

CHAPTER TWO

Babyhood, Period 2[1]
The Story of a Smile

Our baby in about the first month of his life has built up his earliest simple habits, peculiar to himself alone, and he has formed in his mind a significant but blurred picture of the small world around him.

His random reflex movements, in that short time, have trained him to guide his mouth to a nipple by touch or to recognize his bottle as something from which to drink. He will have formed various patterns of crying. He will cry one way to denote discomfort or hunger. If in great discomfort he will scream. Sometimes, now, he will begin to whimper for nothing in particular except the pleasure of the feeling it gives him: combined feeling and sound bring him comfort. Soon he will learn to croon and get placid comfort from that too.

SIMPLE SPIRAL PATTERNS OF LEARNING

During the next two months the baby, almost imperceptibly at first, begins to stretch some of his actions just a little beyond pure reflex movements. He extends them into becoming patterns of learning that are slightly more complex than simple responses to chance external stimuli. He is no longer satisfied with simple reflex actions for survival nor, in fact, with reflexes to give comfort, although now, and all through his life, they will continue to serve those purposes. Reflexes now begin to serve another purpose too. They bring him interesting things to do. Let Stuart illustrate one for us.

For Stuart, clutching a shawl that touched his hand soon ceased to be an isolated incident. There came the day when he clutched the shawl by chance and the clutching gave sufficient pleasure for him to prolong the process. He gripped again and again. He involved every muscle of his body in the effort. Soon it became an impulsive pattern of repetitive gripping that could have seemed to the casual observer to be quite useless. Such an observer would not have been taking into account the fact that there was more in Stuart's actions than met the eye.

[1] This chapter is based on Jean Piaget, *The Origin of Intelligence*, Chapter 2.

Stuart. Repetitive clutching.

Stuart. Reflexive response to a sound.

As well as the obvious physical movements Stuart's activity also involved repetitive messages passing through his nervous system to and from the brain.

Such clutching is a classic sign of the intellectual development of the second period of babyhood. Concurrently other similar repetitive patterns build up. In Stuart's case they included continuing to drum with his feet on anything that they happened to touch. When a sound caused him to roll his head to the side he continued to roll it repetitively, rubbing a somewhat bald patch on the back of it. When he tried unsuccessfully to respond to his mother's speech and merely blew a bubble he continued to blow more bubbles for the fun of it. He played repetitively with his tongue and with his saliva.

Let us look again at Stuart's gripping of the shawl, which he attempted with feet as well as fingers and continued until a sound to his right caused him to roll over and point in its direction.

Until that moment his activity seemed to be a never-ending 'grip – release – grip – release – grip'. But we must take the mental activity into consideration. This makes us change the pattern that we need to consider into 'grip – absorb pleasure from it – release – absorb pleasure – grip'. It continues thus in a circular pattern triggered off by the first reflex response to a casual touch. The pleasure is assimilated into his whole nervous structure, together with all the feeling from the movements, and it is recorded in the brain. Practice makes perfect! Stuart goes on with the circular activity until he has learned quite a lot about what he can do with his hands and not a little about his shawl.

But this is not really the whole story. We have not considered one further modifying factor.

At each 'grip – assimilate – release' Stuart's learning through the experience increases. He starts each new round with a greater knowledge than he had as the groundwork for the round before it. Each time he knows a little more about what to be prepared to experience. It would thus seem better to change our pattern once again, replacing our circle by a shallow spiral. Nothing in life can ever be exactly repeated for it is always influenced, however minutely, by what went before.

Piaget accepted the term 'circular reactions' for such models of intellectual activity from Mark Baldwin and other psychologists. Yet Piaget's research, more scientific than theirs, has revealed within the model far more reason for intellectual growth than the others ever suspected. To keep that point uppermost in our minds, it is probably easier for the average reader that, in this book, we should use the word 'spiral' to describe the form as we watch it grow through its three stages of complexity across the rest of babyhood.

Even in this first stage of the spiral pattern we see a tremendous advance take place in the baby's learning. Although he is still only in the second period of babyhood, he is widening the scope of his habits so as to find pleasure and to learn. What do we all do when we experience pleasure? We smile. And so the baby's mother sees his first radiant smile. Most of his smiles over many ensuing months will be for her, for most of his pleasures will come through interaction with her and from the spiral patterns of behaviour that he builds in her company. An attentive father

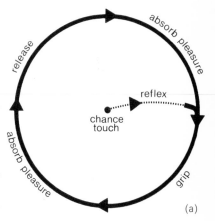

(a)

Simple spiral pattern of learning.

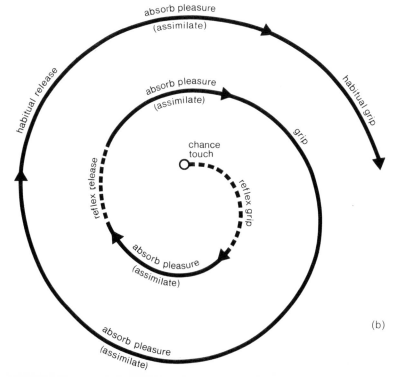

(b)

29

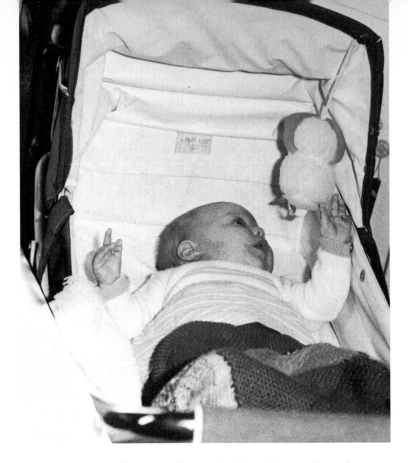

Amber. Hand and eye coordination.

can ensure many smiles too and so can brothers, sisters and grandparents. As we get deeper into this second period of babyhood and as the first stage of the pattern strengthens, even his own hand may earn a smile as he makes it repeat what it is doing. This is not as ridiculous as it may seem. One must remember that egocentricity still prevents him from sorting out 'self' from the rest of his world: all objects and all people are mere extensions of himself.

Through such patterns of activity a child in the second period of babyhood learns to exercise his senses of sight and touch in support of each other. Amber illustrated this for us. It was in the middle of this period that her hand happened to touch a string of woolly balls that were dangling from the roof of her baby carriage. Her eyes focused on them when she tried to grip them. She found gripping difficult, because they moved at her touch. She continued to touch them, as they passed her hand, and to try to clutch them. It all obviously gave her great pleasure, for she smiled at them. Then she let the dangling toy pass and concentrated on her hand, smiling at that too. At last she relaxed, her hand dropped and touched her mouth and, contentedly, she sucked her thumb.

Marieke, towards the end of this period, as her first picture on p. 18 shows, had difficulty in clutching a string of plastic rings that was pressed into her hand. The programme of clutching was activated throughout her nervous system so she clutched the air repeatedly with her legs and toes

Alexandra suspecting her own influence.

as well as clutching the toy with her fingers. It was all one integrated pattern of clutching, passing through brain and limbs.

Alexandra, a few weeks older than Amber and Marieke, shook her baby carriage in a vigorous effort to welcome her mother whose voice she had heard. But her mother did not approach. Then Alexandra noticed that a toy was swinging. It was well out of her reach but she could not know that. She clutched with her hand but, of course, failed to grasp the toy. She tried to talk to it. She punched the air. We could not be sure whether she was beginning to realize that her activity was keeping the toy in motion, but that seemed unlikely as she soon relaxed and quietened. If she had continued we should have thought that she had reached the third period of babyhood's intellectual growth.

Neither Amber, Marieke nor Alexandra could set any of their patterns of activity into motion at will. Each had to trust to a reflex movement of arms and legs and eyes or to adult help.

INTERPLAY OF PHYSICAL AND MENTAL GROWTH

All these simple spiral activities lack foresight or intention so they cannot yet be considered to be intelligent. They lay foundations for intelligent behaviour in the next sub-period.

31

They strengthen the responses that can come from any sensuous impact. They plant the seeds of play.

We see a child sucking for the sake of sucking even when he is not hungry. His eyes learn to focus, at first not with binocular vision so not in depth. We see him gazing at objects that pass before his eyes, as Amber's ball did or as his bottle might. Each time he tries to begin a spiral activity with them. Perhaps he only manages to point.

As the weeks go by he starts up spiral activities with the interesting foot that is making rhythmic movements within his focus and tries again and again to grasp it. He cannot know that the foot is part of himself, but he knows that what he is doing is enjoyable and he smiles.

When his sense of sight or smell tells him of his mother's approach he may put every muscle of his body into a vigorous whirl of spiral activity, long sustained. His wide, welcoming arm movements start up and his legs kick. With luck he blows bubbles as his tongue and throat muscles are brought into action. He feels the interplay of all these activities and absorbs the thrill. If one of them has a chance effect on the vocal cords and causes them to make a sound, or if the gentleness in his mother's voice stimulates a reflex that brings forth sound, he may start a spiral of playing with his voice. On later occasions a repetition of any one element in that spiral will precipitate him into practising it all again. It will be more than a year before he is able to speak recognizable words, but he is feeling the pleasure of sociable conversation as if he could do so now. This is the seed of the spiral pattern that will grow into speech.[2]

And so we see that through these simple spiral patterns of exploratory behaviour a child learns by reacting to everything that comes within his orbit. Above all he reacts to people, especially to his mother. But we must be cautious in our enthusiasm. These first spiral patterns are only enrichments, by repetition, of reflex actions. The child in this period cannot start them off at will; he must rely on a basic need or on a chance encounter to arouse the first reflexive response each time. He will respond reflexively whatever the reminder is. For example, if he is hungry he will suck his bottle whether you present him with the operative end or the reverse end for either will arouse the spiral pattern in him.

Now he is forming habits not only for survival but also for the joy of a learnt achievement. As each learnt pattern becomes more familiar it also becomes neater and the learning grows deeper.

Those of us who care for his intellectual growth will give him small toys to watch and to clutch and will supply interesting sounds for him to hear. Above all we must give him our time and attention. So we multiply his chances for enjoyable learning: equally we increase our own pleasure and *our* learning too.

---

[2] So far we have spoken of the baby conventionally as 'he' or 'him'. At this point it must be mentioned that recent research is moving towards demonstrating that, because of the 'y' chromosome, girls generally perfect speech patterns earlier in life than boys.

FOR THE MORE SERIOUS STUDENT
SENSORY-MOTOR PERIOD, SUB-PERIOD 2,
PRIMARY CIRCULAR REACTIONS

1 The more able student will have recognized that spiral patterns are the outgrowth of the earliest schemas (of Chapter One) as they are further fed by assimilation and accommodation.

2 Piaget uses the technical term 'primary circular reaction' for what the previous part of this chapter has called 'simple spiral patterns of learning'. Essential features are:

(a) They are initiated by *chance* reflexes. Hence they cannot be considered to be intelligent but only to be precursors of intelligence.

(b) They are repeated for extended pleasure and for learning.

(c) They are the child's first *acquired* adaptation to his environment.

(d) Through them two or more of his senses concurrently can cause him to experience satisfaction.

3 While Piaget has accepted the term 'circular reaction' from Baldwin and others his research into the reaction's growth is more scientific than theirs. Piaget gives more emphasis to the child's building the pattern of learning for himself (as contrasted to merely gaining factual knowledge) and absorbing experiences into his whole system. He speaks of a circular reaction as a 'repetition of the cycle which has been actually acquired or is in the process of being acquired'[3] and which 'prolongs the reflex exercise and has the effect of fortifying and maintaining . . . a sensory-motor whole with new results pursued for their own sake.'[4] In other words, the child adapts through accommodation. For Piaget, therefore, epistemology, or the science of learning, has a physico-biological dimension quite as strong as its mental dimension.

4 Circular reactions are sometimes called *conditioned reflexes* or *acquired associations*.

5 It has been implied in this chapter, although not specifically mentioned, that a child in this second sub-period of intellectual development seems to have no consciousness of things continuing to exist once they are out of range of his senses. To him they are quite ephemeral. Piaget says the child only achieves 'elaboration of the "object"'[5] much later on.

6 The smile is an acknowledging recognition of what the child is seeing or feeling. We shall see a contrast to this in the next period.

7 We must be cautious about one important fact. None of the learning so far described involves any clear thinking on the child's part, but only vague ideas that are the life-giving seed for future thought and for future intellectual skills.

[3] Jean Piaget, *The Origin of Intelligence*, p. 49.
[4] *The Origin of Intelligence*, p. 66.
[5] *The Origin of Intelligence*, p. 264.

CHAPTER THREE

Babyhood, Period 3[1]
'A Will of His Own'.

In expounding any part of Piagetian theory it is difficult to talk in terms of ages, for it is normal for children to progress at very different rates. It is the sequence of development that we are studying.

With that caution in mind one could say that in a period that stretches between the ages of roughly three months and roughly eight months a baby shows spectacular intellectual development. Most parents take delight in watching it. They see their child developing more and more character of his own, in contrast to being the almost helpless small creature that he was so short a time ago. Too little do many of them realize what tremendous mental agility as well as physical prowess is growing in him. Both the physical and the mental growth, integrating with one another, give him the confidence to become characterful.

The spiral pattern of learning activity, which we saw at its first stage in the previous chapter, takes on an interesting development at this intermediate stage in its growth. The development is merely a pause for thought. That pause brings the dawning of intelligent study.

THE ENRICHED SPIRAL PATTERNS OF EXPLORATORY BEHAVIOUR

Did Alexandra, in Chapter Two, suspect that her punching and kicking activities were keeping the swinging toy in motion? We shall never know. She was poised on the edge of the two periods. So let us turn to Marieke instead.

Marieke, at just over three months old, had often cooed with pleasure at seeing toys dangle from the roof of her baby carriage. Like Alexandra she had stretched and kicked with the enjoyment. It had all happened through purely reflexive movements. The whole activity had been of a simple spiral pattern.

Then came the day when she noticed the toys slow down and stop swinging. She watched them for a second or two, but the urge to kick was still in her. She kicked again and noticed them swing. In a natural pause

[1] This chapter is based on Jean Piaget, *The Origin of Intelligence*, Chapter 3.

she saw them stop again. She grew solemn. Reflexively she swayed towards them and they moved once more. She had more control of her arms than in the previous period and she stretched both arms towards the toys with a vigorous movement. The swinging accelerated. Then she paused and watched the decreasing motion of the toys. As an urge in her made her wave and kick once more, she received a satisfying feeling of being the cause of revived swinging. A sense of mastery swept over her, exciting her to repeat the whole process, including the pause. Could it be that her own activity *caused* the swinging? She experimented purposefully, pausing thoughtfully to watch and find out. Again and again, with obvious serious intention, she went on repeating the now enriched spiral pattern of behaviour with precise, rhythmic movements, always pausing to study the result of her activities. Then when she was sure of her conquest her smile came.

Day after day she practised at intervals, rolling herself into contorted shapes as she struggled to make the interesting spectacle last.

This could seem a small advance in learning until one realizes that, for the first time, thoughtfulness and intention had entered the pattern and these were the first sproutings of truly intelligent behaviour. Of course, her thinking had not included the contribution of the baby-carriage springs to her achievement. She expected to have the same success when she repeated the behaviour pattern within her more rigid cot (as in her second picture on p. 18).

From now onwards our diagram of spiral behaviour must take on an enriched shape. The pause for thought must now appear in it. And the

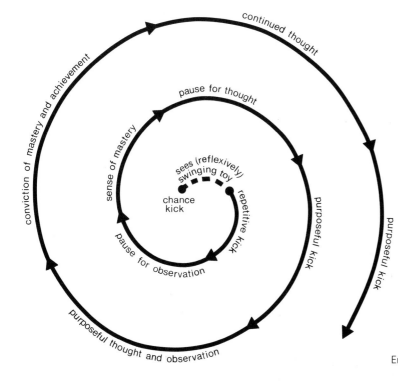

Enriched spiral pattern of learning.

Matthew, convinced of his own mastery.

Ruth explores the feeling of her own feet.

element of chance can be eliminated from it. For now the child has learned how to apply a *known* means to achieving a *known* end in many situations. This is very different from having to wait for a chance disturbance of a toy and the chance of one's arm and eyes focusing in the right direction. The child has thought. He has studied. Now he can re-enact the whole familiar pattern at will. Intention can, in future, be his starting-point. Study, thought, intention, all make this newly enriched spiral behaviour pattern a first intelligent action instead of a random or habitual one. The whole model[2] is both physically and mentally more mature than it was before the pause developed.

During the long spell of this period of babyhood many such spiral patterns of learning are enriched in this way. They become ever more varied and ever more daring. Progressively the learning becomes quicker.

We read of Piaget's son learning to pull a chain to make a toy swing.[3] When he first pulled it he showed fright, but he studied and soon learned to enjoy the achievement. He even pulled it, and was puzzled at failure when the string had been cut below the toy. He had no eye for the mechanics of it; he just enjoyed the process. Soon he was pulling whatever cords he found anywhere. Matthew, at the same age, found similar fascination in jangling a bell on a rope.

Amber, at five months, discovered how to pull her blanket over her head.

Ruth set up an enriched spiral activity between her hands and her feet. The learning involved throbbed right through her, yet she sometimes gazed intently at her clasped hands and feet and learned still more. Gradually she must have come to know that her feet were part of herself.

[2] 'Model' in the dynamic, mathematical sense.
[3] Jean Piaget, *The Origin of Intelligence*, p. 163.

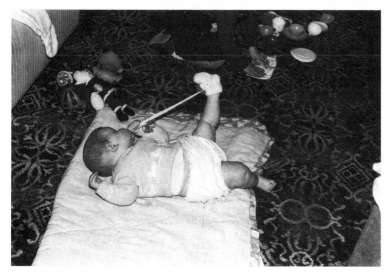

Alexandra coordinating hand and eye.

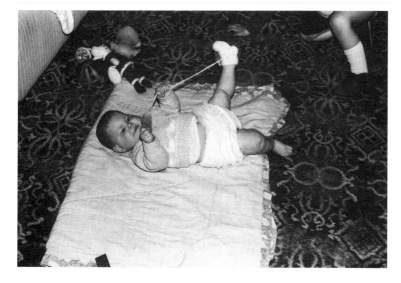

Alexandra, extended study.

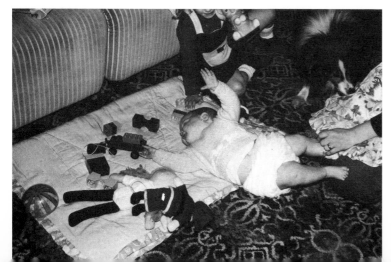

Alexandra follows removal of a toy.

Amber 'talking' with her mother.

Amber greets a visitor.

Alexandra first set up a simple spiral pattern of grasping the tassel of her bootee when it passed before her eyes and her outstretched hand. Soon she learned to coordinate the movements of hand, eye and foot so that she could play this game at will. When the tassel came off in her mouth it called for extended study (see previous page).

Over a period of a few weeks she learned to keep any interesting object in view as it moved. She trained her eyes to follow it. Hence, when her mother took her truck away from her and tried to 'hide' it behind her head, Alexandra followed its course with eyes and hand until her back was curved in a beautiful arch: with a tremendous stretch she retrieved her toy. It was easy to hide it from her completely a minute later. When, before her eyes, a cloth was dropped over the truck while she was moving her hand towards it, the truck disappeared not only from her sight but from her mind.

COMMUNICATION

The joy of communicating exists at any period of learning. As can be expected, it enters the enriched spiral patterns too. It will be dealt with more fully in Chapter Nine but it must be mentioned here. We have seen Amber, before she was a month old, attempting to talk to her mother and to keep a conversation flowing. Perhaps this was her first simple spiral pattern of behaviour. It soon became firmly ingrained, based on arm gestures as much as on mouth and tongue muscles. From that day onwards Amber continually enriched the spiral pattern and quite soon the pause broke in. During each pause she watched her mother's face intently: probably it seemed to her that she herself caused the movements and sounds that her mother's face was making as, indeed, indirectly she had. Amber achieved glorious sounds and enormous bubbles. It was not long before she transferred her conversation temporarily to any visitor who surprised her by entering the room.

THE RECOGNITION OF SIGNS

It cannot be long now before a baby's study of cause and effect will lead him to form a vague, even if at times incorrect, notion that all things that happen in sequence must be responsible one for the other. Even in the previous period the sound of her mother's voice told Amber that her mother was probably approaching. Her father's laugh proclaimed that he was near. It was all confusing, for egocentricity still made her parents part of herself anyway. It was just their ministrations and activities that their voices foretold. As she recognized signs of these ministrations, such as her bottle or bath water, she welcomed them.

But she recognized some signs, even if they were connected with her mother, as foretellers of unpleasant happenings. Like all the other children in our story she soon knew that the tucking of a large napkin under her chin foretold that an unpleasant drink was to be administered. All these children probably saw any napkin as causing the unpleasant taste that was to follow. All of them at first resisted the drink and then, on later occasions, resisted the napkin before the drink even appeared.

Amber, genuine discrimination.

Discrimination

There are other signs, too, that could mislead us. A whole conglomeration of signs (such as the activity of preparing milk, the bottle and the particular welcoming grip of her mother's arm) told Amber that she was going to be fed. But the wrong end of the bottle was put into her mouth. Something had gone wrong within the pattern that she was accustomed to! She was only able to react with a wriggling grimace. Perhaps she would soon have done as Marieke did and reject the bottle with a nimble flick of her hand.

We saw early discrimination in the case of Christine in Chapter One. This example is subtly different for it involves an adaptation of thinking on the part of a child who has *mis*read signs.

The hidden toy

There are still other signs that a child registers in his mind by the end of this third period of babyhood. They are greatly involved with things that he has learned to chew and to suck through his newly enriched spiral pattern of activity.

When he entered the third period of babyhood all things were, for him, ephemeral. While he had them they were indistinguishable from himself: when they disappeared from his range they ceased to exist. Gradually, as we saw with Alexandra, he would try to retain them by following them with his eyes. If they then disappeared he could do no more. But a few months of studying their potential and their parts, through his spiral explorations, gradually taught him to see a part of his toy as a sign of its continued existence.

Mark, recognizing a sign.

Mark demonstrated this for us. He was normally refused the privilege of playing with his sister's puppet which attracted him enormously. We almost hid the puppet beneath a cloth, with just the tip of the stick showing. He probably recognized the stick as a sign that the puppet was there, for he crawled towards it and pulled out the toy. It is unlikely that he wanted the stick for itself alone.

This is a normal Piagetian test[4] for monitoring a child's progress towards recognizing that objects have permanent existence. At this point Mark still needed that one small, clear sign to help him to keep the toy in his mind.

We shall study this theme further in the next two periods.

Things to be sucked

Probably the baby's first very well-known pattern of enriched spiral activity and learning is that of sucking everything he can bring to his mouth. He has always sucked most things that have touched it.

It is not until the beginning of this sub-period that he can bring his hand from any distance to grasp objects that attract him. From that point onwards it is not long before he can bring them to his mouth.

[4] *The Origin of Intelligence*, p. 222.

Quite early in his life any child's thumb chances to come to his mouth and, by reflex action, he sucks it and gains comfort from it. It builds in him a simple spiral pattern of sucking and from that he soon progresses to bringing the thumb to his mouth at will. There is very little need to pause for study as the learning through touch goes on all the time. Nevertheless he occasionally takes out the thumb, looks at it and smiles in recognition.

When, in time, he chances to have a toy in the hand, the toy is brought to his mouth: of course he sucks that too. This also gives him comfort. Gradually he explores all parts of the toy through chewing and gnawing and occasionally looking at it. He enjoys learning from it.

Over the next few months he forms the pattern of carrying to his mouth everything that comes to hand. Gradually he learns that all things have shape and form. Until this time his teddy bear was just an amorphous, warm, comfortable mass: now it has feet and ears, frequently chewed, by which he can recognize it.

Chewing had been one way, even if forbidden, by which Mark had learned to recognize the puppet by its stick.

Daniel even formed a pattern of bringing his feet to his mouth. It all started as an enjoyable occupation when he was in his bath. Wet feet were interesting things to see waving before his eyes and he grabbed one and chewed it. As days wore on the pattern matured in him. Pauses for learning were not obvious, for he studied each foot by sight, touch and taste while he chewed it. Occasionally he broke off and gave it a steady look. There was something different about this foot from other things that he chewed. He could feel it at both ends of himself! Was it part of himself? He could not get this double-feeling experience from his teddy bear!

This has only been an introduction to sucking and chewing for it is in the next period that the activity will almost dominate the child's life and learning.

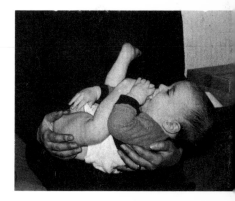

Daniel integrates all his senses.

The enriched spiral learning patterns of the third sub-period, of which sucking and chewing is just one, may take five or more months to mature. They are worth the effort on the child's part. They are worth the patience on the parent's part. For in that five months the child becomes an intelligent human being, laying a path for wisdom and self-sufficiency in his life as a whole.

FOR THE MORE SERIOUS STUDENT
SENSORY-MOTOR PERIOD, SUB-PERIOD 3,
SECONDARY CIRCULAR REACTIONS

This sub-period is significant for:

1 'secondary circular reactions'. The student should keep it clearly in mind that they involve the application of a *known* means to a *known* end. This leads to a discovery of cause and effect.

2 what Piaget calls the systematic 'coordination between vision and prehension',[5] which enables the baby to manipulate objects in this secondary circular way.

[5] *The Origin of Intelligence*, pp. 155–6.

3 the consequent *interest* and *intention*. (Contrast 'intension' which Piaget analyses (with Bärbel Inhelder) in *The Early Growth of Logic in the Child*.)

4 the first stage of the concept of the 'object'.[6] The coordination of hand and eye, together with further exploration chiefly through sucking, helps the child to become so familiar with coordinate parts of some objects that he can begin to suspect the continued existence of a whole object through parts of it that act as *signs*. So what Piaget calls 'elaboration of the "object"'[7] or 'the concept of the "object"'[6] begins to form in his mind. It should be watched during its next two stages.

Thus *signs* of things or of happenings begin to have meaning for the child. The development of this mental advance should be watched in the following sub-periods for, later, understanding of signs will be related to the ability to use symbols.

5 Piaget calls the secondary circular reaction 'reproductive assimilation'.[8] (He speaks of constructing 'procedures to make interesting sights last'.[9]) It involves organization of both assimilation and accommodation. In the past, objects have been assimilated into the child's mind, as, for example, into the primary circular reaction. Now it is entire behaviour patterns that interest him and that he absorbs – not just the properties of objects.

6 This point will be of interest only to the reader who has sufficient mathematics to have studied the theory of mathematical 'groups'. For that reason it has not been mentioned in the earlier part of the chapter, but the serious reader will find groups (in the mathematical sense) in most of Piaget's books, particularly in *The Growth of Logical Thinking: From Childhood to Adolescence*.[10] It is of particular importance to any student training to become a teacher of mathematics or of any science, or, in fact, of any subject that rests upon clear logical thinking. At the risk of over-simplifying, one might say that a mathematical group is composed of mobile elements that interact upon one another without changing the total value of the group, and are capable of returning to their original form. Piaget speaks of 'schemata of displacements capable of returning to their point of departure'.[11]

Piaget's research demonstrates that mental activities in the adult's mind work (almost or quite subconsciously) in the negating and compensating way of elements in a mathematical group, as the mind solves logical problems. He considers secondary circular reactions, with their recognition of cause and effect and their return to an appropriate starting-point, as being the child's first *perception* of 'group form'. But it is perception only and far from understanding. It is hardly a conscious perception and will not be handled by the brain alone until adolescence. A serious student who turns to reading Piaget's epistemological works will meet this theory at all stages of intellectual growth.

[6] *The Origin of Intelligence*, p. 222.
[7] *The Origin of Intelligence*, pp. 263–6.
[8] *The Origin of Intelligence*, p. 365.
[9] *The Origin of Intelligence*, p. 185.
[10] with Bärbel Inhelder.
[11] *The Origin of Intelligence*, p. 156.

CHAPTER FOUR

Babyhood, Period 4[1]
'For him the World is essentially a Thing to be Sucked'[2]

GATHERING TOGETHER OUR IDEAS

In this transitional period of a few months no new spiral patterns of learning behaviour are formed. Yet it is a significant period in itself for strengthening and interlinking the existing patterns in a way that involves genuine intelligence.

The period is a pause – a pause for reflection. It is like the pause we take when we learn no more new strokes at golf for a time but go on practising the old ones. As we practise we give them more serious thought than ever before. This makes us realize that the particular iron-and-stroke combination that we had learned to use for getting out of a shallow bunker could be used beneficially, if unconventionally, for getting a well-placed, short-distance shot from the fairway neatly on to the green. This is a near-analogy but not a perfect one. There is the subtle difference that during our adult pauses we use logical reasoning to foresee possible results: in contrast, in this one long pause the child only practises and interlinks existing spiral patterns of behaviour through an apparent foresight that is, in reality, just sheer hope. He then accepts whatever results come his way. Nevertheless, by trial and error, he learns to use each of his spiral activities to help him to achieve a further purpose. Piaget speaks of 'the logic of values or of action'[3] taking over from reliance on chance.

So, in the pause, the child practises and continues to perfect all that he has learned so far. He extends his patterns of learning to new as well as familiar situations. He links patterns together to serve each other. Above all he continues to practise communicating with adults whom he knows well and, increasingly, with strangers.

He has begun to crawl. He practises that and uses the skill to further his other purposes. He has learned to stretch towards things that he sees, to grasp them and to bring them to his mouth. He continues to bring to his

---

[1] This chapter is based on *The Origin of Intelligence*, Chapter 4.
[2] Jean Piaget, *Six Psychological Studies*, p. 10.
[3] *Six Psychological Studies*, p. 58.

Amber looking for a sound.

mouth and gnaw anything that is available. He grows to love novelty and turns over every object so as to explore and learn every part of it with his fingers, eyes and gums. He listens to any sound the object might make. Amber, at ten months old, repeatedly searched under the disc of a toy record-player, apparently trying to find the sound!

Perhaps a knowledge begins to percolate that objects appear different from different points of view; no longer can the child be fooled if you offer him his bottle at the blunt end. 'Small', at the climax of this period, was so slick at turning the nipple-end to his mouth that we quite failed to get a photograph of the action in spite of several attempts. His hands, as they grasped the bottle, recognized the operative shape from whatever angle the bottle was pressed into them, and he manipulated it at speed without even glancing down at it.

An hour in the life of 'Small'[4]

Let us look at 'Small', in the middle of this period, using his crawling to enable him to grasp, his grasping to enable him to suck, his sucking to explore. His sucking becomes an activity predominantly for learning rather than for feeding. It becomes another classic example of interlinked spiral patterns of learning. And there are many other similar combinations of existing skills that 'Small' used to satiate his inquisitiveness and his love of novelty.

We followed 'Small' with a camera for about an hour in this crucial period, as he pushed from forming new patterns of learning and

[4] 'Small' — a pet name (from *The House at Pooh Corner*, by A.A. Milne) given to Andrew.

concentrated on consolidating and integrating existing ones. He was in slightly, but not completely, unfamiliar surroundings but was with adults that he knew well. There were no other small children to distract his thoughts.

During that hour he grasped and gnawed nearly thirty objects at great speed, paying particular attention to the novel ones, and occasionally returning to his mother to chew her trouser-leg. Whenever possible he manipulated each object to explore it with his gums, at both ends and all angles, so as to find out as much as he could about it. The beach-ball almost defeated him. He lunged at it repeatedly, occasionally managing to grasp it with his arms long enough to give it a fleeting lick before it again slid away from beneath him.

The objects he gnawed during the hour included toys, cotton-reels, a ring of keys, balls of various sizes, the camera (spreading saliva lavishly over the lens), its flash unit and leather case, the leg of a chair, a cushion, a spoon, a comb, a waste-paper bin, a pencil, a notebook, a spectacle-case, the rim of a hat, the corner of a low table, my hand (which, towards the end of the hour he seemed to have spotted as the surreptitious provider of suckable things), the watch that ticked on the appendage to that hand and an interesting knob that he found in an awkward corner at the side of the radiator. With every one of them except the cushion he immediately set up an enriched spiral pattern of exploration through sucking or gnawing, manipulating and pausing for thought.

For further illustration of 'Small's' intensive use of his inbuilt 'teaching aid', the first he ever used and the one that had never failed him, it seems sufficient to let three of the photographs, with only simple captions, speak for themselves.

'Small' and the classic enriched spiral pattern of learning by sucking.

Another hour a month later

It is more apparent than ever, during this period, that the baby enjoys to the full all the elements of any spiral activity and not just the results of it. The activity itself and the experience it initiates become all-important.

'Small' long ago had formed a pattern of drumming with his hands on anything that he found easy to strike, first of all only on cushions and soft objects. This was obviously a simple spiral pattern of learning. It had become an enriched spiral pattern once he began to pause in the activity to look at the dent that his hand had made. This urge to drum on objects, in pauses between sucking them, had remained with him right through to this present period. But he had had to rely on chance proximities to start him on such activities.

Of course when an upturned waste-paper bin was placed within his crawling range he drummed on that too. At first he simply enjoyed the added glorious sensation of the sound and he laughed with delight. Soon he began drumming and pausing, obviously listening to the sound and then to the silence. Ultimately a far-away look that came into his eyes showed clearly that he considered, contentedly, that he alone was the cause of all the noise. When someone removed the bin slickly from beneath his hands he showed utter surprise for a few seconds as he found himself drumming silently on the softer surface that had replaced it. He

'Small'. Enriched spiral pattern of learning through drumming.

recovered quickly and crawled after the bin, then drummed once more. He persisted many times, whether we removed the bin from him or him from the bin. For a few moments, when he was pulled on to his mother's lap, he continued to drum in mid-air. Then he struggled back to the bin.

When there was no doubt in our minds, or in his, that he had achieved mastery over the bin we decided to test whether we could interest him in trying out a new means of getting the sound: we pressed a spoon into the palm of his hand. At first he found it to be just a delaying encumbrance and his face took on an anxious look as his left hand was thwarted in its purpose. He broke off temporarily to suck the spoon (as he had been doing before he found the bin), then happily discarded it and drummed once more.

He had learned a great deal from just that one experience, for when we pressed into his hand a small plastic box, which he had previously sucked and had enjoyed manipulating, he clutched it by reflex action but, as can be seen in the picture, it flew into the air as he raised his arm to drum. The pattern of activity that he had built for himself to enjoy could not be broken by any outside agency nor could *his* interests be diverted to *our* new ideas. The mastery, the experience, the completed pattern of action were what mattered to him at this time.

These two hours, a month apart, in the life of a child in the fourth period of babyhood illustrate the change of emphasis that takes place in the child's learning pattern. Gradually, as his intensive study of objects gives him confidence in his knowledge of them and of their properties he turns the emphasis of his exploration to a concentrated study of the purposes that he can make such objects serve. But the change is only of emphasis, for all through his short life learning has enveloped entire processes. We have consistently stressed this point. His learning has always been wider

'Small' failing to use a tool.

'Small' rejecting a tool.

47

than his conscious interest in the toys through which he has learned. Now it becomes deeper too, as his interest in processes overtakes his interest in things. Nevertheless, both interests will stay with him all his life.

INTEREST IN PROCESSES ACHIEVED BY HIS HANDS

A child of this age will have studied his own hands and feet more than anything else. That has been apparent from the second period onwards. Now he begins to find ways of putting them to interesting uses too. We see him gently opening his hands and watching them as they let an object fall. It is particularly interesting to see him in his bath still gazing at his hands when a slippery bar of soap has dropped from them. Days or weeks later he will watch the soap as it falls. Later still, in the fifth period, he will watch the path it takes as it falls or as he throws it experimentally.

Yet a parent needs generally to be cautious about what the child's true interest is, for that may not be what it seems.

Rosemary had, for weeks, been engrossed in the process of throwing. Yet she rarely threw anything when she was conscious of being watched, so photographing proved difficult. For at least half an hour one day Rosemary's mother and I waited impatiently while Rosemary sucked toy after toy and then threw them only in the occasional split-seconds when our eyes turned elsewhere. Suddenly, at one such moment, the accompanying photograph was snapped. When it was printed it made us wonder. Rosemary was not studying her hands or the trajectory of the plastic ring she had thrown. She was watching her mother. The process that she was enjoying and studying was that of keeping the attention of the adults. After all, apart from food and physical comfort, her mother's attention is her most basic need.

Rosemary throwing to attract attention.

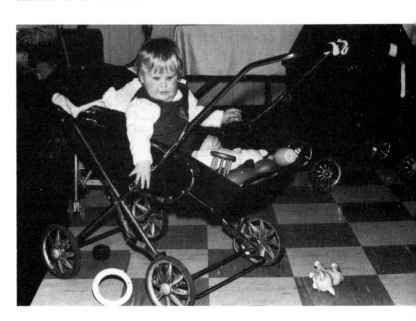

Clive, however, was definitely interested in the throwing process and watched intently to see where each object fell. When he had emptied the baby carriage of at least a dozen toys and parcels from his mother's shopping he flung his leg over the side in his effort to retrieve them for throwing again. He was caught just in time. A few weeks later, like 'Small' in the next chapter, he was throwing experimentally and watching the trajectories.

The enthusiasm with which an unusually alert child in this period may practise hand movements for new and undeclared purposes can take us unawares. For some weeks Derek had been exercising hand grasping and releasing movements in pulling, pushing, dropping and throwing. Then he watched for his chance and, with a lightning movement, pulled out his grandfather's dentures. Since he had a particularly indulgent grandfather this was rewarding enough for it to become quickly (but very temporarily) a practised pattern of behaviour and of study. Visitors had to be warned not to smile or laugh if Derek was on their knees. Though I had been warned, I wanted to see how far Derek would carry his experiment. Knowing that it would take the skill of a dental surgeon to remove my teeth I sat beside Derek and laughed. He pulled hard and persistently at my bottom teeth. After a first few attempts he paused and made a symbolic biting gesture with his own jaws, paused again, bit again, then pulled once more. His wails of frustration at having his most recently acquired and enjoyable behaviour pattern completely fail could not possibly have been interpreted as a compliment to my teeth.

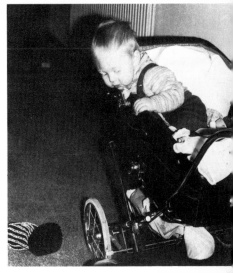

Clive throwing to study results.

THE HIDDEN TOY: SECOND STAGE

The interest in processes, over and above interest in the objects that play a part in those processes, runs parallel to the child's acceptance that objects can continue to exist when they are out of range of his sight and other senses. Through his integrated activities he begins to study them in their spatial relationship to one another. He no longer considers them only in relation to himself. No longer does he need (as Mark did) to see the stick handle of a puppet protruding from its hiding-place to be persuaded that the toy is still there and still desirable. Gravely he watches you put it in its hiding-place, knows that it must be there out of sight, lifts the covering or dives beneath it, brings out the toy and triumphantly sucks. 'Small', unfortunately not photographed until the next stage, did just that.

Has the time come, then, when you cannot hide from him something that you genuinely want him not to have? – especially if, at the time, you have only one hand to spare! Try the following experiment while he watches. Let us presume that you have his toy and a cushion and a rug. Hide the toy first under the cushion. He retrieves it. Hide it there a second time and he will retrieve it again. Now take it from him again and, while he still watches, pop it first under that same cushion and then immediately transfer it to beneath the rug. He will still only hunt in the first place. For another month or two he will be unable to cope mentally with more than one hiding-place at a time.

RECOGNITION OF SIGNS

Take again the first example of simple hiding and finding. The child has not merely ceased to need the sign given by a puppet's stick to tell him that the puppet is still there. His advance in intellect is greater than that. He has accepted a whole visual pattern into his mind. The cushion is part of that pattern. It can remind him of the whole pattern, including the movement and activity. Hence he can be sure enough of what lies beneath to lift the cushion (which does not interest him) in order to obtain the toy (which does).

Now he will also be able to read more complicated signs. We learn of Piaget's daughter,[5] Jacqueline, at as early as nine and a half months old, liking fruit, which she associated with a glass dish, and disliking soup, which came from a china bowl. She always opened her mouth for the former and kept it firmly closed against the latter. There was no need for her to watch which was coming, for the sound of the spoon on glass or on china was a sufficient sign. This nonchalance was her downfall, for her mother soon thought of tapping a spoonful of soup on a glass dish before administering it to Jacqueline, who had not even given it a glance.

APPLICATION OF KNOWN MEANS TO A NEW END

Many reminders, including signs, stimulate a child in this period to more complicated behaviour patterns than were previously possible. We see that he has a rudimentary foresight for what he expects to achieve. In Derek's case he could even symbolize it. It suggests, in a way, that the child almost senses the abstraction of a movement when he cannot achieve the movement itself. Derek wanted *my* teeth, so *he* chewed. Piaget gives a neater example. His daughter, Lucienne, in the fifth period, had been unable to open a matchbox, so she opened and closed her own mouth several times: it was as if she could anticipate the opening action irrespective of the matchbox or her mouth.[6]

In every instance we have a child applying one existing spiral pattern, or more than one, to acquiring and studying a new, desired end. We see him absorbing the result into his thoughts and registering the total complicated process into his whole being once he has modified it to serve his ends. We see him constantly widening his environment by such very simple experiments. As he continues through the period, all these movements become ever more controlled and more venturesome.

As the enriched spiral patterns interlink and blend with one another in this way, they cause other developments too. Soon we see the child at times obviously playing and at other times ritualizing (e.g. pretending to sleep), and he often imitates sights and sounds in so far as he can. Most noticeable will be his imitation of the rhythm of the rise and fall of his mother's voice. These imitative skills will be considered in the second section of this book because they mature only later, during toddlerhood.

[5] Jean Piaget, *The Origin of Intelligence*, p. 249.
[6] *The Origin of Intelligence*, p. 337.

FOR THE MORE SERIOUS STUDENT
SENSORY-MOTOR PERIOD, SUB-PERIOD 4,
COORDINATION OF EXISTING PATTERNS

1 The student must be careful to remember that this is still a sub-period of only primary plus secondary circular reactions: the child is now experimenting with interlinking them.

As the world around him becomes wider and more interesting, showing him many things to be desired, any interlinkings, such as grasping and sucking, will bring him fuller enjoyment of a toy. It will bring both familiar and unexpected results. It arouses in him a desire to get even further unfamiliar results and to find novel ways of satisfying more of his desires.

2 The sub-period is a first level of structured achievement as the child moves from reliance on reflexes to completely intelligent behaviour.

He develops the foresight to hope for a new experience, but he can only apply his existing circular reactions in trying to attain one.

3 The interlinked circular reactions show:

(i) Obvious *intention*, including the element of unreasoned foresight.

(ii) *Search* for known means that could be subordinated to the unforeseen end; i.e. there is no dependence on chance reflexes.

(iii) *Application* of a known schema for other than its known ends denotes that the child has mentally to consider possibilities in relation to one another.[7] This is certainly an act of intelligence.

One might add that he would no longer pull a broken cord: he would by now notice that it was broken and useless.

4 The second stage of an 'object concept' is another sign of memory strengthening and of a child subconsciously accepting that an object has permanent form. He sees that objects exist in relation to one another and not just to him. But he can only carry in his mind an immediate experience concerning them. Further complications are beyond him.

5 Recognition of signs grows stronger. Symbolic imitation begins (as in Derek's symbolic jaw action, which Piaget might also attribute to an impulsive invocation of magic). It is an *abstraction* of a possible desired achievement.

Elsewhere Piaget makes much of signs and symbols. The essential difference between them is that a sign (e.g. the puppet's stick or the sound of a spoon on china) is external and recognized by the child, whereas a symbol is created by him. This study will be extended in Chapter Ten.

6 Accommodation. The word 'absorbing' was used on page 50, line 32. Piaget's technical term would be 'accommodating'. This fourth period is one in which accommodating to the particular in a situation, in contrast to merely assimilating the general, increases rapidly. It results in modifying existing schemas in the light of new experience.

The Origin of Intelligence, p. 211.

CHAPTER FIVE

Babyhood, Period 5[1]
A Year of Curiosity

It is difficult to decide whether to talk of the fifth intellectual period of babyhood as beginning at about ten or twelve months of age, for not only is there a wide range of development noticeable from child to child but also for any one child there is a transitional period of a month or two during which he slips gradually into the fifth period. This fifth period may last anything from ten months to a year although it is by no means one of slow intellectual growth.

The characteristic mark of the period is yet another, this time complete, maturation of babyhood's distinctive spiral patterns of exploratory learning. It is a period of learning to study processes. Before taking this final look at spiral patterns we need, however, to note that quite early in the period the baby will come completely to terms with the permanent reality of objects wherever or however they are hidden.

OBJECTS FULLY CONSERVED IN THE MIND

The exploratory examination of objects, which we watched in the previous two chapters, continues at first unabated. Objects will still be manipulated. In the early part of the period they will still be chewed. Quickly, now, this manipulating and chewing convinces the child that objects are real and that they can be moved to many places even when out of his sight and out of reach of all his senses. They can be held in his mind neatly in relation to other objects. They can be desired. They are worth hunting for and worth retrieving.

This is a different mental attitude from the one described in babyhood's third period, when the child needed a sign such as the puppet's handle to suggest to him that the puppet still existed. In the fourth period he certainly unearthed the toy from a simple, immediate hiding-place but could carry no complications in his thoughts. Now let us continue the game of the hidden toy.

'Small', at the beginning of this new period, was still exploring every object within reach and carrying most of them to his mouth. On the day

[1] Chapter based on Jean Piaget, *The Origin of Intelligence*, Chapter 5.

'Small' retrieving pencil from its only hiding-place.

we next tested him we noticed that a favourite toy seemed to be a pencil so, while he watched, we hid that pencil beneath a hat. 'Small' retrieved it with such speed that we carried him a few yards away (still sucking the pencil) before taking it from him and hiding it again under the hat. Then, while he still watched intently, we transferred it immediately to beneath a cushion. 'Small' was bemused for a moment and studied the situation. He crawled over and lifted the hat, glanced at the floor beneath it, then carried the hat with him as he wriggled forward to dive under the cushion. He retrieved and sucked his pencil.

Later that afternoon, when we thought he had had time to forget the exact pattern of the incident, we tried it again. Because of 'Small's' gift for lightning speed we waited for him to go to the far end of the room. Once more, while he watched, we hid the pencil beneath the hat and immediately transferred it to beneath the cushion. This time casting no further glance at the hat, he launched himself straight at the final hiding-place and retrieved the pencil.

In case the first experiences had left him with a lurking memory, which we had failed to consider, of the cushion as the ultimate hiding-place, we tried other pairs of hiding-places too. There was no doubt about it. It was the pattern of action that he had learned and not just the particular example. We transferred the object several times, sometimes even returning it from an apparent final to a mid-stage hiding-place. Always he went straight to the correct destination. At one time I even suspected, probably without justification, that he was enjoying the spirit and challenge of the game. We were certainly satisfied that he could carry in his mind, concurrently, the toy and several hiding-places and that he could distinguish between them.

'Small' investigating both hiding-places.

'Small' searches only in the ultimate hiding-place.

From that point forward a parent can help such a child to consolidate this new skill by playing hiding games with him. Soon the time will come when he will hunt spontaneously for a desired, lost toy that he has not, in fact, seen to be hidden. Whether the need to hunt is adult-initiated or self-inspired, the baby will enjoy adult participation and certainly the participation of other members of the family.

This growth of conviction in the permanency of objects helps the final shape of the spiral activity to mature. It is in this period that it comes to its climax.

MATURE SPIRAL PATTERNS OF EXPLORATORY LEARNING

Since spiral patterns of exploration and learning are the hallmarks of babyhood's intellectual growth, it may be well to glance back at their development so far before looking at them in their final form.

Spiral patterns did not make their appearance in the first month of babyhood. They first appeared as cornerstones of learning in the second babyhood period as simple and almost incessantly repeated movements (such as gripping) that were triggered off by reflex actions. They became the baby's first habits. Although the baby was absorbing knowledge and skills from them there was no obvious pause for thought.

In the third period of babyhood the patterns matured considerably. It was particularly significant that a pause for thoughtful study broke into the cycle. Although each activity owed its origin to a chance reflex (or to adult initiation) any repeats of the initial activity became intentional. In the pauses for study and thought the baby began to rely on mental activity as much as on the more easily observed physical parts of the spiral. Consequently he began to realize that he could manage to achieve a well-known end by applying an equally well-learned means to that end. This marked the beginning of intelligence as such.

In the fourth period the spiral patterns gained strength although they took on no change in form. In many cases they were interlinked. In many cases, too, the well-known means to an end were applied experimentally. This often gave surprising results.

Now, in this fifth period of babyhood, we see a complete maturation of the form of the spiral pattern (although interlinkings of that final form will enrich it still more in the period yet to come). It is a significant enough development to justify its growth lasting for many months.

By the end of the fifth period the baby will no longer be confined to using *known* means of achieving either expected or unexpected ends. He will begin to use trial-and-error procedures to try out entirely original means of creating interesting situations. He will still, of course, be unable to foresee what the results of his experimental activities will be, but, whatever they are, he will study them with obvious interest.

The pauses for study will remain in the spiral pattern, but their purpose will be increasingly the studying of whole processes rather than the study of the results themselves.

This pattern of behaviour showed its first sproutings earlier when we watched the child studying the activities of his hands. Now he goes on to

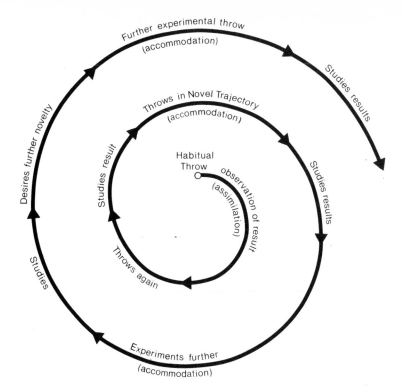

Further experimental throw
(accommodation)

Studies results

Throws in Novel Trajectory
(accommodation)

Desires further novelty

Studies result

Habitual
Throw

observation of result
(assimilation)

Studies results

Studies

Throws again

Experiments further
(accommodation)

Mature spiral pattern of learning.

find out a great deal about what those hands can do, about how they do it and about what processes other objects in the environment can be put through. In the whole study, covering pauses and active moments too, he will observe, consider unforeseen results, then frequently modify his further activities.

This all comes about partly because the year-old child once more finds a rapidly expanding environment as he begins to enjoy the experience of walking. He finds more things than ever before to be curious about. This development is bound up with the fact that he now sees everything in his environment as having a permanent existence and having a relationship to other things around it. Once he has made a comparatively brief inspection of something new, his need to continue to suck it evaporates and his interest increases in what purposes he can make it serve. He is fascinated by processes and decidedly more interested in them than in mere objects. True curiosity has been born. He is conciously wanting to learn for learning's sake.

Perhaps the most characteristic and most incessantly repeated example of this new, mature form of spiral exploration is the activity of throwing in varied trajectories. Infuriating as it is to many a harassed parent, this is the outstanding way in which a child of this age learns.

Just as we gave special attention to purposeful clutching as the outstanding example of the spiral patterns in the third period, so we will now look in some detail at the learning that can be observed as a child explores the joys of throwing in interesting ways.

THROWING IN EXPERIMENTAL TRAJECTORIES. 'SMALL' AND SHEENAH

We will let 'Small' have the final word about spiral patterns of learning in this period, except that it cannot exactly be a word because he could not talk intelligibly at the time. Yet he could experiment with trajectories in the fully mature spiral patterns that this chapter is concerned with.

As soon as he began to walk no object was safe with 'Small' around. He had developed the classic schemas of dropping and throwing and had just found the joy of rolling a ball across the floor and chasing it.

The day came when, after a few minutes of such play with a ball, he paused, looked thoughtfully at a spent computer tape, grabbed it and hurled that too. Fortunately he was sitting on the end of it so the tape unwound as it sped along, creating glorious curls behind it. Joyfully, 'Small' chased it along its course. No adult could have resisted giving him another spent tape which he hurled, equally joyfully, in the opposite direction. The same happened to a third which was shot with even greater vigour.

'Small' enjoys an enriched spiral pattern of learning.

While the adults cleared up and settled to a rewinding session 'Small played with other toys, but he was only too anxious to start again when presented with the rewound spools.

Up to this point the pattern of spiral activity had been the half-mature one typical of babyhood's fourth period, coordinating existing behaviour patterns, such as grasping, throwing and following, while at the same time studying the objects involved.

With this same well-worn behaviour pattern he hurled the next spool and laughed as he chased it. Then came the experiment typical of the fifth period. He became still and thoughtful for a moment and then threw the last spool with a sideways action in an entirely new direction. He sat silently and studied the results and then held out his hands for another spool. Certainly that was a better solution from his point of view than trying to rewind his handiwork! This spool he also hurled sideways. The next was sent spinning forward into the air.

Of course we gave him more. But the game suddenly turned to real chaos when a five-month-old puppy named Sheenah joined in. We had arranged for her visit (without expecting this exact setting for it) in order

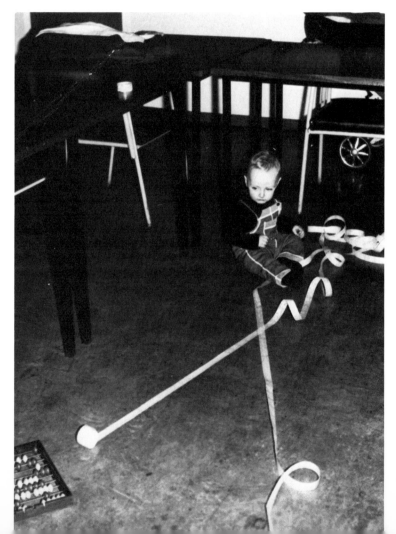

'Small' investigating by a mature spiral pattern.

'Small' — complete pattern of filling and tipping.

'Small' vies with Sheenah for a ball.

to watch the child's reaction to his first encounter with a puppy as much as to watch the dog's earliest encounter with so young a child.

For the first moment or so they took no interest in one another at all. 'Small' glanced at Sheenah and turned to filling a box with oddments and pouring them out again. Piaget [2] had recorded that new experiences have no impact unless they have factors common with mental patterns already formed. Yet it seemed incredible that 'Small' should show such lack of interest in so adorable a puppy as Sheenah. Sheenah, for her part, effusively greeted the adults, who were already her friends; then she sniffed around at the toys on the floor. She picked up a toy as it fell from 'Small's' box and brought it to me. I led her back to give it to 'Small'. She did so, licking his hand with gentle friendliness.

As far as 'Small' was concerned, Sheenah now became a live toy whose reaction he could absorb into his scheme of playthings. He liked the soft warmth of her tongue, but was thwarted by not being able to grasp it. He liked Sheenah's sheer size, her proximity as she rubbed against him, the softness of her fur. To all these things he responded with simple reflex actions. Then the toys, which he could dominate, won the day. He returned to hurling a computer tape. Sheenah chased it. For both of them toys were more fun than socializing.

That was when chaos ruled supreme. The room became a whirl of flying toys and computer tapes, of an excited puppy whose claws slid on the slippery floor as she bounced to greet her new-found friend, and of a baby lunging eagerly to clutch a dog in his arms or to grip its ever-licking tongue with his hands.

It was the adults who tired first. Sheenah was dragged unwillingly away. 'Small' responded contentedly to a cuddling from his mother. I was left to tidy up the room.

Such classic examples as these last through the fifth period of babyhood. Exploratory throwing is definitely a pleasurable mature spiral pattern of experimenting with processes.

Many a mother sees it as naughtiness and scolds her child as she retrieves precious packets of shopping that have been thrown from baby carriage to pavement. In desperation she straps him more tightly into his seat to prevent him from leaning precariously over the side in his eagerness to watch the packets fall. And in the early morning when his cries waken her, not because he is hungry or uncomfortable but because he has thrown toys, pillow and blankets from the cot, she may well catch him in an experiment at climbing over the bars to retrieve them. If she replaces them in his cot does he show gratitude by accepting them for themselves? No! Immediately he hurls them out once more to study the curved movement of their flight.

What advice can a developmental psychologist give to such harassed parents? Try to cease to be harassed? Become interested instead? It will be easier to be patient if you *are* interested. Study the signs of his gradual advance towards increasingly more hazardous throws, as he learns from each experience and as he modifies the next throw accordingly! It is worth the backache. Give him more to throw? Yes! Of course, make sure that he

[2] Jean Piaget, *The Origin of Intelligence*, p. 275.

cannot throw your breakables and foodstuffs nor things that might annoy passers-by. If you anchor a selection of toys, each with a long string, to some part of the baby carriage his interest in their anchored fall will be just as great and he will learn just as much from their trajectories as if they were free. And remember, he will be studying you and your friends too and the ways in which you pick up his jettisoned toys.

The mature spiral pattern will urge him to do other things that harass you. Inquisitively he will open any container that comes his way. He will climb precariously, sometimes to 'see over' and sometimes just for the joy of the experience. He will pile up objects to climb on.

You may soon find yourself broadening your own interests as you look for yet further examples of his mature patterns, or, shall we say, of his first truly experimental behaviour. As he builds castles of bricks or of sand you will understand why he knocks them down again immediately: he is learning from the total process of feeling a motivation, building, studying and knocking down. There would be a yawning gap in his learning if he did not complete the whole circle. You may be amazed at how quickly he has learned to fit together interlocking plastic rings to create a tower. Do not be too disheartened if he dismantles it before you, his proud mother or father, can point it out to your visitor. *You* may be interested in his tower or his achievement; *he* is interested in the process, including the destruction.

It might interest you one day in the summer to walk along a mile of a seaside stretch of sand and count how many one-and-a-half-year-old children are helping to build sandcastles and how many are knocking them down. The numbers should tally reasonably well.

And why, you might ask, is it important that my child should study throwing all his and my possessions and that he should demolish sandcastles? Apart from the fact that he is learning to experiment, there are two further answers. The first is that he is beginning to study positions and movements in space which are elements of pre-geometry. The second, and more significant, is that he is starting to form patterns of thought that will give him skill and confidence in reasoning as he grows through childhood to adult life.

A CAVEAT

Certainly all this progress must lead any parent to feelings of cheerfulness. Yet sudden progress imposes an increasing load on parents just as it did in the third sub-period. This time the increased load is twofold. *Directly* there is the need for tremendous and cheerful patience. *Indirectly* there is the need for a parent to have alert foresight in training the child to habits that prevent him from disrupting the normal life of the general public.

His newly formed interest in processes and experimentation may induce him to delay you a thousand times on every walk or shopping expedition while he examines (and perhaps experiments with) each new find. Or perhaps he insists on slowly putting on his own shoes (possibly on the wrong feet) when you are hurrying to receive visitors. His egocentricity still convinces him that *his* interests are *your* interests. A year of experiences has taught him to expect full cooperation from one who cares about his intellectual growth.

But there are limits! This sense of cooperation maturing in him is no bad thing to encourage as long as you take this ideal chance of making it a two-way process. He is interested in processes. He wants to find some for himself but he is prepared to be taught others. He is instinctively keen to cooperate with trusted adults. Such adults, if they cultivate their own foresight, can profitably harness and interlink for him his interests in processes and in cooperation.

He need not be allowed to insist on getting (oh! so slowly) on to a bus unaided as he holds up a queue. Parental foresight can prevent him from stopping in the middle of a busy pedestrian crossing to play with his toy car. If he is left to do these things they are not intuitive expectations of cooperation: they are a complete ignoring of other people's needs, in fact of other people's very existence.

Such tendencies come at a time when it is particularly opportune to train the child in cooperation. At this time he is keenly interested in studying the individualities of all things, especially of people. He likes people easily. So he is also particularly receptive to suggestions a parent may make about other people. It ties up with the current spiral pattern of exploring processes: cooperation is one such interesting process. And the sixth period, yet to come, is an excellent time for consolidating it.

A suggestion such as, 'Here comes the bus. Let me lift you on so that the other people can get on quickly too', can seem to him to be a positive invitation to an experiment.

The word 'positive' is used advisedly. It will be several years before he can at all understand the negative[3] equivalent of '. . . so that we do not keep the others waiting'. There is no point, therefore, in expecting him to respond to suggested correction once he is eager and poised and has started to concentrate on mounting the bus by himself. It is for this reason that constant parental mental alertness and foresight, producing *advance* positive suggestions, are all-important. With good prompting he will develop scores of such cooperative gestures which not only help the 'other people' but also arouse in the child a further line of learning just when his intellectual development is ripe to receive it. The end of this period is a ripe moment, too, for beginning a systematic training in simple expressions of gratitude. He can become genuinely interested in a giver as well as in a gift: thanking that giver completes the process.

So a happy early training in good citizenship begins in a truly practical way and ties in nicely with his natural spiral pattern of learning about processes. This study of processes will prove to have been a turning-point in his whole intellectual advance. In the future, powers of scientific investigation will stem from it.

FOR THE MORE SERIOUS STUDENT
SENSORY-MOTOR PERIOD, SUB-PERIOD 5,
TERTIARY CIRCULAR REACTIONS

1 This is a sub-period of discovering new means through active experimentation.

[3] Jean Piaget and Bärbel Inhelder, *The Early Growth of Logic in the Child*, Chapter 5.

2 There are three major elements in the tertiary circular reaction.

(i) The child begins to search for new and untried methods of creating unusual situations.

(ii) He is studying activities rather than objects.

(iii) The third stems from the two others: he now wishes to learn for learning's sake rather than for material results. Piaget says tertiary reactions are 'no longer due to simple reproductions of fortuitous results but to . . . a search for novelty as such'[4] or 'an effort to grasp novelties in themselves'.[5]

3 The child's acceptance of 'object reality' was essential before this interest in processes could overtake the interest in objects themselves.

4 Foresight. The child begins to foresee new starting-points worth trying out. This helps him to study the variations in any general pattern of cause and effect that he has already accepted.

5 The results of his experimentation bring in new evidence which he *interiorizes* to enrich his existing schemata, expanding them or modifying them. So, as assimilation and accommodation go on, the schemata grow in power. Later in this book (in Chapter Eight) we shall examine more closely the changing balances of power that can occur between assimilation and accommodation: these variations will be seen to cause the demarcations between *play*, *work* and *imitation*.

6 The serious student should take note of the reference (p. 60) to a baby's inability to understand *negative statements*. He can be trained harshly to expect a slap on the hands as he recognizes an angry tone of voice in the command, 'Don't touch that.' But this mechanical response is not an understanding. He can only *understand* and later conceptualize what he has taken into his schemata through *positive* experience. The growth of ability to handle negatives is dealt with in great detail in Piaget's works (with Bärbel Inhelder) *The Early Growth of Logic in the Child* and *The Growth of Logical Thinking: From Childhood to Adolescence*.

7 Piaget pays great attention to dropping and throwing and to the child's use of them in *The Origin of Intelligence in the Child*. References are clear in the index of that book so the serious student should turn to them.

8 We have referred previously to the intuitive pre-growth that later will programme itself into an intellectual pattern of reasoning which has mathematical group form. Such positioning of objects as the pencil beneath the hat out of sight of the child gives an experience that he will 'interiorize' as part of the foundation of this group form. It is also a basis for geometry and algebra in the future.

9 The student should notice that, in this period, the child graduates his experimental movements as he 'tries to ferret out new phenomena'.[6] As yet he has no idea what those phenomena might be (i.e. they are not specifically in his mind).

[4] Jean Piaget, *The Origin of Intelligence*, p. 264.
[5] *The Origin of Intelligence*, p. 265.
[6] *The Origin of Intelligence*, p. 274.

CHAPTER SIX

Babyhood, Period 6[1]
'Monarch of All He Surveys'

It is generally in the last few months of his second year that a child gradually grows out of babyhood behaviour. He reaches the peak of exploration through the almost-closed spiral patterns that are characteristic forms of babyhood learning and he moves towards learning through play and through ensuing toddlerhood skills. In this chapter we will look at the mature spiral patterns at their absolute peak of enrichment. We watch the child demonstrate how nimbly he can exercise these mature spirals, having reached the point of interlinking them with one another, but now with a *specific* hope in view.

The fusion of spiral patterns with elementary foresight may come in a purely visible and practical way, perhaps with obvious pauses for thought. It is rather like the way simpler spirals interlinked in the fourth period. At other times it will be memories of experiences that the child summons up. We shall discern this fusion when, at its climax, it bursts forth as an invention of a new means that he hopes might satisfy a specific desire.

Sometimes the child's experimental solutions serve their purpose: more often they do not. There is still no logical reasoning behind his trial-and-error attempts. They are purely pragmatic interlinkings of perhaps concurrent and perhaps remembered experiences. A chance juxtaposition of materials might catch his eye, showing something so near to a possible solution of his problem that just a slight mental leap forward is needed to produce foresight. With this foresight he takes action (using two or more mature spiral activities) and hopes that the action will serve his purpose. He rarely seems to show regret if it fails to do so.

Piaget's most quoted example of a diagnostic test for foresight is the following problem that he put before his own children.[2] He tempted each child to try to retrieve from outside his playpen a stick which was a little longer than the total width of three gaps between the vertical bars. Piaget always laid the stick on the ground parallel with the side of the pen; the child could easily get his hand through any of the gaps.

[1] This chapter is based on Jean Piaget, *The Origin of Intelligence*, Chapter 6.
[2] *The Origin of Intelligence*, p. 336.

We tried this test on a series of children. The very young ones always made a few futile attempts at pulling on the middle of the stick and then abandoned the problem.

Children in the fifth period often groped laboriously towards success, grasping the stick through the bars first with one hand and then with the other until, quite accidentally, the stick was tilted vertically and came through because it was already being pulled. Such children generally learned from the episode and could repeat it. But their intellectual activity that had led to success was only one of trusting to continuous, frustrated pulling. It was an interlinking of mid-stage spiral activities. The stick was first pulled through by chance. Throughout the fifth period interest seemed to be more in the activity than in a desire to possess the stick, for generally no further use was made of the stick. Those who learned from the episode, however, were nearing the borderline between period five and six.

Sarah, in period six, illustrated how her ability to interlink her spiral activities of pulling and twisting enabled her to study progress and to pounce with insight when she noticed that the stick and the gap had dimensions in common. She had been pulling with each hand in turn for some moments when the stick chanced to tip almost vertically. She paused and studied it, gently tipped it more and more, studying it all the time. From the sheer gentleness of her advance it seemed that foresight had suggested that the stick could be manipulated to fit the gap. When it was parallel with the vertical bars she pulled it through, still gently.

Sarah pragmatically studying a problem.

'Small' did not wait for us to test him with the stick and the railings. He demonstrated to us that he could interlink ideas by means of foresight in solving a problem of his own. He had become rather over-enthusiastic at wheeling about his empty push-chair and the time came when he found that it was literally 'cornered'. He pulled. He pushed. He tried twisting the handle. He paused for study, then tried all these moves again. Then an idea seemed to strike him. He must have remembered that the wheels should turn round. Or perhaps he remembered his old, pleasant 'interiorized' activity of incessantly rubbing the wheels of his toy cars into movement. With added determination and seriousness he set about turning the push-chair wheels by hand. Occasionally he broke off to try a further push on the handle. The fact that he could not succeed was of little consequence to us because 'Small's' trouble really was that an adult had applied the brake. If it had not been for that he would have solved his problems with the use of his mature spiral patterns interlinked with insight. While one adult attracted his attention for a moment the other surreptitiously slipped off the brake. 'Small', still sprawling on the ground, returned to manhandling the wheels and pushing with his shoulder. So he felt the reward of success.

A few days later he provided another demonstration for us. This time it was without success, but it had all the features of interlinking mature spirals with insight. He tried unsuccessfully to open the glass doors of a bookcase that he had often seen me lock. When he felt sure that manual effort was not going to do it for him he looked around for a 'key'. We knew what he was searching for, for several times he twisted his wrist as if subconsciously symbolizing its action. He spotted a ball-point pen,

'Small' inspired by insight.

'Small' willing Scotch tape to fall.

grabbed it and tried to fit it in the lock, although it could not have looked at all like a key. Surely this was foresight – and the invention of a new hoped-for means to a specific end! Earlier that day he had tried to solve a similar problem by symbolization or 'magic'. When he found that he could not grasp patches of adhesive tape that were well above him on a door, he bounced himself to the ground several times to persuade them to fall.

It is amazing how this mental grasping of a situation and consequent invention of a means to an end can grow in a child of this age, when physical mobility is widening his horizons and early speech is helping him to steady his thoughts. An example of Jacqueline's invention of a means to an end is so delicately told by Piaget that it is worth quoting in full as a final example for the first section of this book.

Jacqueline has been wrested from a game that she wants to continue and placed in her playpen from which she wants to get out. She calls, but in vain. Then she clearly expresses a certain need, although the events of the last ten minutes prove that she no longer experiences it. No sooner has she left the playpen than she indicates the game that she wishes to resume! Thus we see how Jacqueline, knowing that a certain appeal would not free her from confinement, has imagined a more efficacious means, foreseeing more or less clearly the sequence of actions that would result from it.[3]

CONCLUSION

What a long way on the road to intellectual prowess Jacqueline and 'Small' and other near-two-year-olds have travelled in this first major intellectual period of their lives – that is, in babyhood! Soon we shall not call them babies but see them as little girls and boys of character.

The spiral patterns through which these babies have interacted with varied environments have served them well. These have been both the hallmark and the backbone of all learning. The child's own senses have been his tools. As each period succeeded the one before it, he has used what he culled from the previous period as a foundation for the next. Gradually his intellect has played a more predominant part in his explorations, helping him to use his senses to greater effectiveness. Ever since his feeble reflexes, on the day he was born, brought messages to his brain he has built up learning by absorbing the essence of experiences into his whole self. Interiorization of both external and internal experiences has induced him to form habits that have become spiral patterns of steadily increasing complexity. All have interlinked and substantiated one another to become valuable learning skills.

These skills will never be abandoned. Very soon now he will become able to apply them intuitively in carefree play, not always showing the strong urge towards 'finding out' that has been so noticeable in the last few months. Yet the learning will still be there, even if less obvious to the observer. Play will predominate over the struggle to learn. Through play the child will learn. In toddlerhood he will learn even faster than in babyhood. In each succeeding intellectual period that awaits him he will learn faster and more fully than in the one that preceded it, unless his urge to learn is starved or impeded. That is the next part of the story.

[3] Jean Piaget, *The Child's Construction of Reality*, p. 297.

FOR THE MORE SERIOUS STUDENT
SENSORY-MOTOR PERIOD, SUB-PERIOD 6, INVENTION OF NEW MEANS TO ACHIEVE ENVISAGED ENDS

1 This must be seen as a transitional sub-period between babyhood and toddlerhood. In epistemological terms it is transitional between the sensory-motor and the preconceptual periods.

2 During this sub-period tertiary circular reactions continue, increasingly in linked form. There has always been a growing element of serious thought in both secondary and tertiary circular reactions, but to the uninitiated observer the physical reactions have seemed more vivid. In this final sub-period it is probable that, because of the increased proportion of thought to action (remembering that thought is quicker than action), mental schemas combine, creating foresight. The experimentation that we are accustomed to seeing becomes 'mental combinations' and before trying them the baby *foresees* a possible solution. 'Thereafter the contrast between the empiricism of simple groping and the intelligence of deductive invention seems to be complete.'[4] Piaget would say that sensory-motor schemata had gradually become interiorized to become 'operations' (in the mathematical sense).

3 A reference was made in Chapter Three (for the sake of the mathematically minded reader) to the mathematical 'group' pattern of mental reactions.

The mathematically minded observer can watch examples of this being strengthened in many of the flashes of insight shown by babies in this period. Piaget quotes the example of a child immediately running round a sofa to retrieve a ball that had run under it: he had not waited to look for it beneath the sofa. Obviously the three-group pattern had formed intuitively in his mind. There is another story of Piaget's son dragging his father round a wall when a gate would not open. We found at least one example of a child of less than two climbing over an obstacle in search of something that had gone under it. A mathematician will recognize that all these instances have group form.

4 Most children in this sub-period acquire an ability to comprehend symbols given by others. This is partly due to ideas gradually penetrating their minds about symbols that they notice repeatedly and partly due to flashes of insight. It is further evidence that some of their activities are mentally controlled even though we see them as physical achievements.

5 One can, therefore, see a connection between the fifth and sixth sub-periods in this way. In the fifth sub-period a child learns to study processes; in the sixth, having interiorized some processes, he can bring them forth as the roots of insight to solve others. To help the mental operation he may symbolize his ideas.

[4] Jean Piaget, *The Origin of Intelligence*, p. 341.

Introduction to Section II
Toddlerhood

In the final chapter of the previous section we watched a baby, during the last few months before his second birthday, pass through something that is akin to a metamorphosis. He emerges from babyhood into a self-assured, self-opinionated, highly mobile and generally cooperative, though sometimes obstinate, toddler. His most outstanding characteristic is his ceaseless expenditure of abundant energy.

His natural hunger for learning by exploring his environment will continue unabated throughout about three years of toddlerhood. His *ways* of learning, however, will take on new and more complicated forms which are speedier and more economical of effort than the spiral patterns of babyhood. The spiral patterns have served their two main functions. They have fed skills into the intellectual growth of babyhood and cemented the innate desire to learn: they have laid down foundations of knowledge upon which all future learning will be built. Sometimes in the future we shall see their characteristic shape peeping through the complex patterns that are overtaking them in their usefulness. None of us ever quite abandons them. Throughout life each new set of mental skills that we acquire (while still retaining the old ones) enables us to learn at cumulative speed. Toddlerhood skills are no exception. They are exciting for the child who uses them, and for the attentive parent who watches them in use, because the speed of learning that they show is so apparent.

The one characteristic of the child's outlook that changes only marginally is egocentricity. It will still remain strong throughout the period of toddlerhood, although it becomes steadily somewhat less total. As it decreases, his interest in and reliance on adults becomes wider, although a long-term full sense of security comes only from his parents. The child who is most confident of constant parental proximity becomes the one who now, and throughout life, is least precocious and is most relaxed and sociable with adults in general.

He learns which people he can expect to make him happy: he studies them particularly astutely and lavishes his friendship on them. With them, almost as with his parents, he practises his earliest sociable habits.

Before abandoning babyhood he has worked out in his mind the separateness of himself from material things. As he manipulated and explored objects he attempted to dominate them. During toddlerhood, even more slowly, he must learn to recognize the separateness of *thought* between himself and his mother. One sign to us that this is happening will be his occasional good-tempered efforts to dominate even her too, at times by bouts of sheer obstinacy.

I remember clearly one instance of the onset of such obstinacy.

Derek, who was just over three, was a happy, active and malleable child, and a very bright little boy. One day he, his mother and I were going out to dig for peat. The three of us had reached the stage of picking up appropriately sized baskets and spades, going to the garden shed and donning heavy, shabby shoes. Derek looked critically at his yellow wooden spade and said, 'Not this spade. I'll take the red one.'

In vain his mother and I tried to persuade him that the yellow spade was better. Each time he said quietly but firmly, 'No! The red one!' Ultimately his mother exclaimed, 'Look Derek! If I go into the house for the red spade I shall have to change my shoes.' Derek, who could not know that time was on his side, nevertheless stood firm. His mother changed her shoes and as she entered the house he whispered to me, with a mischievous glint in his eyes, 'And she will have to change her shoes back again too!' From the calm, quiet way he handled the whole matter and through the pleasurable sparkle of mischievous enjoyment, it was obvious that the whole process had been an experiment and certainly not a bout of bad temper on Derek's part. It had all been a surprising, isolated incident from a normally obedient small boy.

This story illustrates how one can help such a child to separate himself from 'apron strings', but one cannot safely force the pace. If the bouts of obstinacy become either bad-tempered or tearful, through frustration from thwarted egocentricity, the pace is being forced too much.

Freudian psychology illustrates for us how damaging excessive anxiety in the toddler can be. It illustrates how such anxiety can be sublimated or 'bottled up'. We know too little as yet about how much *delayed* damage can be done (by forcing the pace of anxiety through imprisoned fears) to the character and mental strength of the youngster both at the time and for the future. Many mothers, with the best will in the world, although against their own instincts and desires, enforce separation upon their toddlers in the name of socialization and for the sake of early academic prowess. Only the toddler himself can demonstrate to you whether and when he is ready for short periods of such separation. And you, the parent, must take into consideration the fact that he has no foresight about time. However willingly, perhaps keenly, he may run in among other children he may, within minutes and certainly within an hour or two, anxiously long for you. He generally learns to sublimate this longing, to 'put a brave face on it', but the anxiety, even if buried, is there.

The long period of mother-dependence and serene interaction with members of the immediate family may well have been the greatest contributing factor in helping human beings to develop brains so infinitely superior in function to those of other animals. Interchange of thought with his mother, not only in speech but at times, seemingly, through something as intangible as telepathy, helps the child to clarify

Gentle socialization.

and enrich his own ideas and to build them into his memory. Let us look at this normal progress in more detail.

Quite soon during late babyhood and early toddlerhood we see a child able, without strain, to play contentedly at short distances from his mother; elsewhere in the house, for example. Those who have had most complete mother-affection will, in fact, gain such confidence as soon as they start to walk.

If such a child ceases to hear his mother's movements for any appreciable time, or if by some apparent instinct he suspects her absence, he will toddle through to check up on her. Gradually his periods between checking up grow longer and his wanderings away from her are extended. Gradually, too, he learns to share her with children other than those in the family. He only accepts this sharing for short spells of time and then only if there are plenty of toys to help him to combat his healthy jealousy. Flora, in our picture, was taken by her mother weekly to visit Jonathan and Matthew in this way. At each visit, all was happiness and serenity, but by the end of an hour socialization always gave way to frustration. Similarly if the periods when his mother is not within range become too long, and if there are too many other people around, whether adults or children, his brain can become over-excited as his anxiety becomes greater than his conscious mind can cope with. Perhaps he sublimates it. Perhaps he becomes morose. Perhaps he becomes belligerent towards other children or destructive of toys or furniture. He may sublimate his anxiety by 'showing off' to a visitor, or perhaps by expressing his lonely thoughts in symbolic play or in his paintings. There can be dozens of such outlets for pent-up yearnings. They are all forms either of sublimation or of catharsis.

How long such sublimated anxiety lies buried before coming to the surface again, perhaps in tantrums when he gets home or the next day, perhaps even in harsh behaviour as far ahead as adolescence, is a wide-open field, still needing much study and research.

In contrast the toddler who has no such anxieties rapidly becomes confident and happily self-assured. He develops true abilities instead of precociousness. It can at first seem contradictory that it is he who is the more likely to extend his exploratory habits, sometimes wandering considerable distances from his parents and coming back contentedly. This venturesomeness is founded on confidence and on an inner sense of security.

David, a two-and-a-half-year-old, was such a venturesome child. He had the run of a very long garden at his home. It ended in strong railings overlooking a main railway line and the entrance to a tunnel. His mother reported that he ran into the house more than thirty times one day shouting, 'Mummy! Train go in dark.' Not much of a vocabulary you might think! No! But he had gained the confidence to go far afield in the course of his study, to study intensively; and, like a good scientist, he was bursting to publish his findings. (Now, as a young adult, he is in fact a scientist.) I use this case as an example of a toddler's contented mind freeing him for wide-ranging exploration, both physical and mental.

Any child like David, who goes through toddlerhood with such serenity and with such ample stimulation for mental exploration and for communicating his findings to those who still seem to be part of him, will make tremendous intellectual strides. The subject-matter of his study matters little. It may be nature study or trains, and with 'Small' (from Chapter Eleven) it may continue to be kitchen utensils and their mathematical shapes. It is the fact that he is learning *how* to study that is all-important.

Similarly it matters little which language the child is learning to use. All languages have structure and it is his learning to cope with such a language structure that is all that matters. I taught for six years in an international school in which the medium of instruction was English. Children of six, whatever their nationality or native language, were speaking English fluently within a few weeks of entering school, although they returned to their native languages each afternoon. They were stimulated to enthusiastic exploratory learning in general and, urged by the need to express their vivid thoughts, they seemed to 'catch' the new language as easily and imperceptibly as they might have caught measles. Children who entered the school at later ages sometimes took half a term or, in a few cases, a term to become fluent. Very few indeed took longer than that. The urge to communicate is a powerful stimulant when a young child has exciting information to pass on. And other skills, besides language, that grow during toddlerhood, such as listening and imitating, support language itself in its growth.

In the next few chapters we shall monitor the main streams of intellectual development that are the skeletal structure of toddlerhood development. Put very simply, they are the growth of prelogical ideas of play (particularly repetitive play), of language, of imitation, of early reasoning and pre-mathematical thought and, ultimately, of memory.

Language includes not only the language of speech but also of artistic expression and expression through music and movement. It encompasses writing and reading. While we have too little space to monitor all these we will at least look at the toddler's thinking as expressed in gestures and in early art. Any toddler of serene mind will handle all these tools of learning concurrently, integrating them with one another, for to him there are no boundaries between them. They are simply 'life'.

Attentive parents, most of them more accustomed to thinking in terms of subject boundaries, will probably find it easier to watch for the emergence of subject-focused potentials in their toddler's intellectual progress. For this reason the remaining chapters in this book are presented as completely as possible along subject lines. At times we shall have to recapitulate in searching for the roots of speech and imitation.

Nevertheless, the reader should always bear in mind that for the child himself progress is in one long tangled line. It can come in its richest form through enjoyable undifferentiated play where the mathematical, the artistic and the linguistic fuse into one. The parent can sway the emphasis of the play by judiciously enriching the environment, but for the toddler the learning will be a tangled web. For him work is play, play is work, enjoyment and exploration. His language is spoken through painting or music or dance or through his lips. In fact all are for him one great, wide, wonderful experience of his small world. All intermingle, building into him learning skills and memories that will coalesce into preconcepts, which are the subject of the next chapter.

FOR THE MORE SERIOUS STUDENT
INTRODUCTION TO THE PRECONCEPTUAL
PERIOD

Toddlerhood is known technically as the 'preconceptual period'. This name can be interpreted in either of two ways. It is the period *before* the one in which the child (of four and a half or five onwards) begins to form simple, dynamic concepts, such as those of number, length, sequence, etc. Alternatively it can be seen as the period *during* which preconcepts are formed. The latter definition seems to be the more obvious one to use as the basis for the rest of this book.

The preconceptual period is one of spectacular intellectual growth. (The word spectacular is carefully chosen: the child's progress is easily *seen* by the observer.) It is equally important as a period of strengthening foundations for future learning.

Learning, in future, will gradually become less spectacular. It should never become any less intense. As learning becomes more internal it is merely less easily observed. Future learning, culminating in the abstract reasoning of adolescence and of adulthood, which is the most rapid and intense learning of all, grows more fully on foundations laid down in a serene, unworried preconceptual period.

CHAPTER SEVEN

Crystallizing Experiences into Tangled Ideas

An attempt has been made so far not to load the average reader with technical terms. At this point introducing just one such term becomes inescapable. It is the term 'preconcept'. The formation of preconcepts through play is the focal characteristic of the growth of intellect in the pre-school child, once he emerges from true babyhood at some time between about eighteen months and two years old.

THE EARLY GROWTH OF PRECONCEPTS

A preconcept is the essence left in the mind and body from a group of experiences that have a common element. Preconcepts are the outgrowths of the spiral patterns of learning that characterized babyhood. They are the images that hold meaning for the toddler; but each image can be vague and insubstantial. Such images are not merely visual. They are the sum total of sediments left by experiences which influenced any or all of the senses. They are thought patterns that motivate behaviour and that are involved in it. They result from a child's subconscious attempts to classify such experiences before he is in fact able to do so. They prompt the thoughts that precede words, or that precede the 'semi-words' that most of us call 'baby-talk'.

A FEW EXAMPLES

You may wonder what jumble of ideas was going on in the mind of eighteen-month-old Jeremy when he first said, 'Foof, foof!' on seeing and chasing after a motor mower that had a smoking exhaust. What peculiar approximate comparison to the mower's smoke, persisting in his mind, made him later apply that same 'semi-word' to a bonfire, then to steam from the kettle — and then later still to a rattling car? The first three had apparent smoke in common, while the mower and car both moved and sounded similar.

Jeremy's interest had been dominated first by the sight and sound of the smoking exhaust, but he had also absorbed impressions from the movement and from the rattling. It was the jumble of such ideas that created the preconcept. A preconcept is dynamic, so this one evoked 'Foof foof!': that in turn enriched the smoke-dominated preconcept and became part of it. Any interesting revival of any part of a preconcept can reawaken any other part of it in his mind. The rattling car did this, although it did not smoke. It made Jeremy gesticulate and say, 'Foof foof!'. His mental struggle with the whole complicated idea was classification in confusion. Until he can conceive a class of things that have a common factor (cars, for example, or mowers), he cannot learn the conventional word to apply to those things; he must trust to 'baby-talk', or gestures, to express the element uppermost in his mind.

Jeremy retained his interest in the mower throughout the summer. By the time he was two he drew it for us – as a scribbled puff of bonfire-coloured smoke. It would have been cruel to dishearten him by asking, 'Where are the wheels?' or, 'Where is the handle?' Wheels and handle had not registered in his mind. The blades had registered: he symbolized them, for his own delight, by waving his arms in rhythmic circles.

Soon after reaching the age of two he had played with a toy mower and had seen enough mowers at work for such machines, through their action and through the job they did, to register in his mind and earn a (conventional) name of their own. It made no difference to him what shape or size or power or colour they might be.

This, of course, has been a specific example from one particular child. For each child examples will be different, plentiful and varied. Any child will imitate any part of any preconcept in any way he can. Imitation and symbolization are his way of coming to terms with it and, together with 'semi-words', may be his major form of language. Those 'semi-words' help him with the confusion of ideas that he is trying to hold in his mind. The world around him is too big to be understood.

Beth, until Hal arrived in her world, had loved her 'Teddy' more than any other small thing. Now she had divided loyalties. She was puzzled. At exactly two she was much too young to distinguish, other than intuitively, between the inanimate and the live. In the week since Hal had come, she had made frequent spasmodic efforts to sort out the turmoil he brought into her mind. When alone with her thoughts, she talked about it in monologue. We listened to one extended monologue when she was strapped, alone, in the back of a car for a ten-mile drive. A few key words, such as 'mummy' and 'baby', dominated what was largely incoherent chatter.

At home she talked to Hal in gestures and in words. She kissed him and offered him inappropriate toys. Teddy was in no way forgotten. When Hal was being fed, Beth found sufficient vocabulary to make it quite clear that Teddy was no such further gift: Teddy needed feeding too. It was Teddy that she took to bed with her. The tangled preconcept in her mind and in her behaviour-pattern gradually reached a more stable form over the next few weeks and months.

As time goes by all preconcepts start to steady in this way. For those that first develop strongly, the child soon learns appropriate adult language: the words that his parents use merge and grow into the preconcept. He may imitate them. 'Go walk' or 'Feed Teddy' are

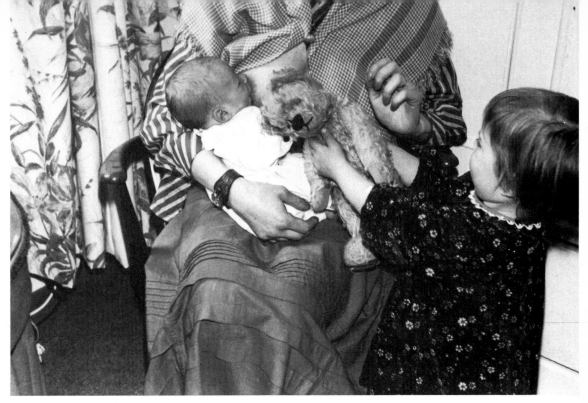

Beth accommodating to new circumstances.

meaningful requests from a two-year-old who has formed rich, mobile patterns of their meanings. But an alert parent may learn just as much about his or her small toddler's thoughts and interests by monitoring his non-verbal talk or his body language, or by examining the pictures that he draws, as by listening to those few precious words.

Such an alert parent will also discover that preconcepts of the very young are wound around specific objects rather than around classes of objects. Piaget tells a well-known story of his daughter Jacqueline, at two and a half years old, talking of 'the slug' every time they saw a slug when they were on a country walk.[1] Piaget asked her patiently and persistently each time whether it could not be a different slug. Her bewilderment made it obvious that the question had no meaning for her. She could not hold a class of slugs in her thoughts, although she could remember one slug. It was not that plurals worried her. If she had seen two flocks of sheep on separate occasions she would have considered them to be the same flock. But seeing only one slug and, at the same time imagining a class of them, when she had *never* seen more than one slug at a time, was beyond her.

These three examples illustrate the fact that for a very young toddler preconcepts are illogical and nebulous, and normally concentrated around the people and things that have had a strong influence on his activities. All are seen from the child's own central point of view. Incidents happening further from him have less impact. As he reaches the middle of the period the emphasis will change, as the story of Paul Daniel illustrates.

[1] Jean Piaget, *Play, Dreams and Imitation*, p. 225.

'Wuzzy'.

PAUL SHANNON Dec. 1911

Paul Daniel, when he was approaching three, still held his own experience as the focal point but, from constant observation of happenings around him and through many conversations, he had enriched his preconcepts to a point where he registered such happenings even if they did not implicate him. He had formed a passion for cars.

At that time I had a green Wolseley car that seemed to him new and wonderful. He came for his first ride in it and he loved every minute. He bounced about, pointing eagerly out of the side window at all the other cars that we met and he gazed out of the back window at others as they drew close to overtake us. For him none of these was quite so wonderful or so fast as the one that now seemed to be a member of his family. He called it 'Wuzzy', which was his approximation of 'Wolseley'.

On arriving home he ran straight to his easel, clipped on a full imperial-sized sheet of paper, grabbed a green felt pen and drew a picture. Since he had been using crayons for six months or more, the shape of 'Wuzzy', as can be seen from the illustration, was fairly accurate. What of all the other cars on the road? In his preconcept of car-travel they were a whirling mass everywhere around 'Wuzzy'. For him they were comparatively less significant than 'Wuzzy' so he drew them smaller and much less distinctly.[2] Paul Daniel was adamant, too, that 'Wuzzy' was the best car because it was the fastest of all the cars on the road. So he drew in plenty of wheels. In fact his picture tells us fairly accurately about his whirling and vigorous preconcept of the ride as a whole, with its colour, movement and speed. Any reasoning shown in the drawing was purely implicit, or, as Piaget would say, reasoning by 'transduction'.

The muddle in healthily formed preconcepts is gradually sorted out as toddlerhood draws towards its close and a very elementary form of logic settles in. Memories are more plentiful and these memories, together with primitive foresight (which toddlerhood logic allows) help the child in his

[2] I could not help being reminded by this of the statue of Rameses II at Karnak with his beautiful but less important wife only high enough to reach his knees.

experiments as he plays. Let us look at Christopher jumping from bales of straw in a barn.

Christopher was a farmer's son. Through all his senses and through the exercise of his muscles he had long ago built up a field of knowledge about straw. He knew of its usefulness for animal bedding and for insulation. He loved its golden colour, its smell, its slipperiness. It is a good weapon in a friendly fight. It is soft and welcoming to fall into. He had registered 'straw' not only in his thoughts but in his whole nervous system.

Now, through impulsive play, he and Neil practised jumping from ever-increasing heights of straw bales. What further preconcepts were brewing in their minds? They noticed that their impact on landing became heavier. Christopher called a halt to scatter the landing-place with straw 'to make it softer to land on'.[3] Then they began to jump in upward and forward arcs instead of cautiously downwards. They experienced height, speed, gravity, impact, all as challenges to themselves.

Simon, at just under three, was probably learning about height in an equally convincing manner.

It is through such play as this that pre-school children who are unhindered or, better still, encouraged to play build preconcepts to the verge of true concepts by the time they enter school.

Christopher forming preconcepts at play.

Simon realistically learns about height.

---

[3] This is an example of logical foresight.

Hannah and a near-concept of number.

PRECONCEPTS OF THE COMPLETELY ABSTRACT

This leads us to look at preconcepts of complete intangibles such as number. If you speak to your child about 'three yellow bananas', how does his mind respond? He can imagine seeing and tasting bananas. He can imagine seeing yellowness. No physical sense can cope with the meaning of three. Such difficult mathematical preconcepts merit a chapter of their own towards the end of this book. But here is a foretaste of it.

Hannah was given the standard Piagetian diagnostic test.[4] Two rows of counters were spread out, correspondingly spaced before her: she was asked if there were just as many in each row and she said 'Yes'. Then the visual appearance of one row was disturbed and the same question was asked again.

Of course a tiny toddler could not have answered either question except by gambling. An older one, who could appreciate the original 'one-to-one correspondence' of the lines of counters, might have answered the first question correctly. As for the second question, more often than not it defeats *any* toddler, for his sense of sight overrules any idea of equivalence. He tends to translate the question into one of length, which he *can* see, or even of density.

What of Hannah's answer? Immediately and emphatically she said 'Yes'. There was almost a challenge in her attitude. It was no gamble, for further skilled questioning could not shake her.

[4] Jean Piaget, *The Child's Conception of Number*, Chapter 3.

Hannah, in her home, had helped her parents in dealing with number situations until the idea of their meaning had distilled in her mind. She not only had a preconcept: she had a full concept of small numbers. And she was still well under school age, so she does belong to this book.

MUDDLED PRECONCEPTS DUE TO METAPHORICAL SPEECH OF ADULTS

One cannot leave this chapter, which dwells heavily on confused preconcepts overruling a child's understanding of speech, without quoting a further experience that should give us warning.

Catherine, in the accompanying photograph, had for several years thoroughly enjoyed attending our college to 'play with Piaget toys'. Her father, my colleague, was apt to joke with people and to tease them. On this occasion, instead of running ahead of her father in the usual way, Catherine entered, hanging behind him and gripping his finger for security. Yet she came in willingly. She sat beside me speechless, with the Piagetian 'mountains' in front of her, and watched her father as he went from the room. She ignored all the toys.

Then, suddenly, she ejaculated, 'When you make me into a guinea pig will it take long?' (or similar words which we failed to tape).

The reader will easily imagine the ensuing conversation, of my trying to put her at her ease and to persuade her that the feat was beyond me. 'Daddy said so,' was her much-repeated response. 'But Daddy was

Catherine dreading life as a guinea pig.

teasing you,' I insisted. 'You know he often teases you.' 'I know,' responded Catherine, 'but not this time. I heard him tell Mummy, "Mary wants Catherine for a guinea pig this evening. Is it OK?"'

It took some time to contact her parents. When her father came and collected her she said 'Good-bye' and even 'Thank you' with great dignity and composure and she departed with a few backward glances and a wave.

The story does not end there. For nearly a year Catherine avoided being alone with me although she liked to visit under parental protection. We never mentioned the guinea pig subject in her presence, anxious as we were to allay what still seemed to us to be lurking fears. Meanwhile Catherine started school.

The climax came one afternoon when I was helping her father and his students to prepare Piagetian tests. Catherine sat beside me and asked, without preamble or explanation, 'Is it right that you could not have done it?' 'Done what?' 'Turned me to a guinea pig?' I assured her that I could not. Then came the outburst, which can only be quoted approximately because, again, it was not recorded.

'Well, I went to Jane Smith's party. And there was a man there and he picked up a bowler hat. It was empty and he made a rabbit come out.' I half sensed a touch of scorn in her voice: that *I* had less skill than a conjurer!

This time, of course, it took only minutes to contact her father. A possible truth that had evaded our thinking dawned on him before it came to me. 'Mary, do you think she was wanting the experience, nervously, perhaps, but *wanting* it? And you failed her?'

This story could stand a great deal of analysis. Throughout the telling it has been obvious to the reader that Catherine held muddled and entangled preconcepts about guinea pigs and fairy-tale magic. It would be a further eight or more years before she would be able to appreciate fully the metaphorical meaning of 'guinea pig'. Had her behaviour during the current year been sublimation or catharsis? As the year wore on we had realized gradually that we were more worried than she was. But we were watching the dictates of her conscious thinking. What was going on in her *sub*conscious? The puzzle about this sort of thinking will be referred to again in the final chapter which is about memory.

THE MOST DIFFICULT OF THE PRECONCEPTS

So far we have looked at the earliest preconcepts of experiences connected with mundane things such as cars, high-jumps, slugs, lawn-mowers and even of guinea pigs! We have seen that, in an imperceptible way, the toddler probes towards the essence of their meaningfulness and of abstract qualities that groups of things or of experiences can hold in common.

We have mentioned, too, preconcepts about less tangible interests in life such as colour. To this we might add preconcepts of size, warmth or time. We have glanced at the intangible essence of number; another concept intangible to the senses is time.

Intervals of time, not time itself, begin to have some meaning for a child towards the later stages of toddlerhood. Yet all of us have had experiences of such unanswerable questions as 'When shall I be five?' or of a toddler's inability to understand the promise, 'Just wait two minutes and I will come.' Derek, one day, was getting impatient for his mother to switch on the television. She said, 'It is not time for *Playschool* yet. It will come in a few minutes when that big hand on the clock gets to there', and she went from the room. Returning less than a minute later she found Derek poised precariously on the fender and moving the clock hand round. His only incipient preconcept of time was of the agony of being kept waiting.

Toddlerhood is thus a time of forming preconcepts. A contented child, active in his play and exploration, forms them plentifully. It is hazardously easy to think of them existing just in his brain or his mind. The brain is certainly their focal point, for the brain controls all bodily functions, but every preconcept has registered its path throughout his whole nervous system and can be triggered into action at any point.

The rest of this section will examine preconceptual growth from the various points of view given in chapter headings.

FOR THE MORE SERIOUS STUDENT PRECONCEPTS

1 Toddlerhood is known in epistemology as the 'preconceptual period'.

2 According to Piaget the formation of preconcepts is the central motivating force not only towards intellectual growth but also towards the development of speech. A preconcept is dynamic. As well as accumulated knowledge it has in it an urge to go forward. One way to go forward is to communicate your excitement and thoughts to others. So in his urge to share his thoughts with his mother the child gesticulates and ultimately speaks. Once he can speak the speech promotes further development of the relevant preconcept: in fact it all becomes an extension of spiral patterns of intellectual growth.

3 Psychologists other than Piaget are divided in their opinions as to whether thought or speech comes first. Vygotski, for example, considers that speech comes before thought. None doubts that the two ultimately substantiate one another. But a preconcept is far greater than speech or thought. It includes them both: each is a store of particular experiences fusing together within the child.

The serious student will easily see that preconcepts are enrichments of the schemata laid down in the sensory-motor period. The seeds of his first preconcepts, for example of his mother (or of his own foot), can be dated back to the time when he first recognized his own individuality as separate from hers.

4 Preconcepts afford fertile ground for the concurrent development of symbolism, imitation, play, work, memory and of early reasoning and prelogic.

5 The student must take two particular warnings from the story of Catherine.

The first is that such a young child blandly accepts the possibility of magic because so many things happen in everyday life for which he or she can see no explanation of cause and effect. It is impossible, for example, for a child of four to understand *why* depressing a switch should cause a light to come on or *why* a needle should jump to a magnet. He is, after all, only four years on the way from the absolute babyhood in which he accepted without question all that happened around him. Magic is not far removed from needles jumping to magnets. We feed such misconceptions with fairy-tales, with Father Christmas and with conjurers, and so we add still further muddle to the preconceptual mind. The easiest course for the bewildered toddler to take is to relax and accept.

The second warning is that one should never expect a child before adolescence fully to understand the use of metaphor. His mind cannot cope with even similes until he approaches adolescence. With a metaphor it takes the adolescent or completely adult mind to penetrate the hypothetical thinking involved. Similarly the fully abstract meaning of such a word as 'reign', in the sense of holding royal office, is beyond him. If you question a child about the queen reigning, or ask him to paint a picture on that subject, even a junior-school child will concentrate on the material concomitants such as wearing a crown or launching ships. Much of children's literature, such as the account of Christopher Robin and Alice as they watch the Changing of the Guard at Buckingham Palace, portrays this outlook delicately and well.[5]

A parent or teacher cannot be expected to go through a dozen years of life without expressing hypothetical thought or metaphor in the presence of children. However, when a child shows complete bewilderment or misunderstanding, or alternatively is misinterpreting what he thinks he understands, the adult can generally look back to what he himself has said and can adjust it.

6 Preconcepts, vague and muddled as they are, are the first tentative recognition by the child of abstractions. They include generalizations held insecurely, and often inaccurately, about such properties as sequence, length, number, speed, common characteristics in groups of things, sharing, equivalents and so forth. They are the roots of concepts which will be formed during the intuitive period and junior life.

[5] A. A. Milne, *When We Were Very Young.*

CHAPTER EIGHT

Play, Imitation and Learning

Once a pre-school child has reached the last few months of babyhood he spends most of his waking hours in play and exploration. When he has gained sufficient language to do so he may well call it work. He speaks of 'helping Mummy to lay the table' or of 'helping Daddy to saw the wood'. Many of the 'helped' ones may well see this as more of a hindrance unless they realize the enormous learning process that they are nurturing in the child by cooperating with him and encouraging such activities, and by promoting conversations about them.

At other times the toddler recognizes play for what it is. He plays just for the sake of absorbing pleasure from it. He concentrates on playing, knowing it to be play. 'What are you doing?' asks a visitor. 'Play in sand,' responds the toddler, in what may be his first approximation to a sentence.

Play, work, imitation, learning are a huge conglomerate of activities, difficult for the adult observer to sort out unless he or she has some guiding knowledge of what key distinguishing points to look for. For the child of about one or two 'imitation' and 'learning' are far beyond thinking about because those two words describe abstractions of which he has never *knowingly* had experience. 'Work' and 'play' can be meaningful words that he often sees applied in practice and which, by the age of two, he applies himself, but they are far too interlocked for him to distinguish between them.

One might challenge this statement by saying that a child of eighteen months, or even younger, often imitates. Yes! But not *knowingly!* And it is an increasingly frequent activity of the two-year-old, which the adult can watch, although the toddler is unaware that he is imitating. He knows what his mind is impelling him to do, but he does not know that he has a mind: he only considers that he is playing.

PLAY, IMITATION AND EQUILIBRIUM BETWEEN THE TWO

How do imitation, work, study and learning fit in with play in babyhood and toddlerhood? Where do dividing lines come? Again we turn to Piaget for a simple decision on this matter.

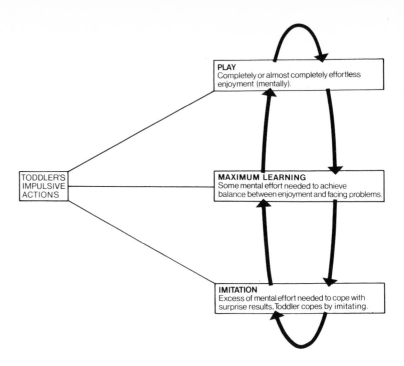

Interweaving play, work and imitation.

All our activities in life create impressions on our minds and on our personalities. In play all or most of the memories that we assimilate are pleasant ones: that is what makes it play.[1] If, however, activities give us some unexpected and surprising results it takes effort on our part to study them, to adapt our activities to the new ideas they introduce and, in general, to accommodate our whole attitude to accepting the new situations. So long as the surprises do not outweigh the easily assimilated pleasure, we accept them in our minds quite comfortably. We easily learn a lesson from the whole, balanced process. Sometimes, though, we receive an overdose of surprises, especially from experimental activities, and it is difficult to accommodate our thinking to all the new ideas. It is then that a toddler attempts to cope with the undigested parts of the experience by subjecting them to imitation. As he imitates he studies them further. We shall meet examples of such almost defeatist imitation in future chapters. It is to some extent a subconscious form of imitative experiment.

Of course, in similar circumstances, babies also impulsively imitate something they want. In their case it is completely subconscious. We saw an example in Chapter Six with 'Small' bouncing to the ground in the hope of persuading patches of adhesive tape to fall from the door (see p. 64). Such imitation is far from unknown in adults: a feeling of insecurity often makes an adult purposefully imitate what he cannot achieve or

[1] Diagram simplified from that in the introduction to *Play, Dreams and Imitation in Childhood*.

cannot understand. But it is in toddlers that imitation is generally most obvious to the observer.

As in the case of all intellectual development the pattern is slightly more complex than so far described. Play, learning and imitation all interact with one another.

Imitation intermingled with pure symbolic play helps the growth of creative imagination. Such interaction is something that we must study. Through other interactions we get varying forms of play and imitation.

The sum total of all categories of play and imitation helps the child partly to clarify what is in his mind, to get something of a balance into his thoughts and gradually to sort out and strengthen his preconcepts.

PIAGET'S THEORY OF THE GROWTH OF PLAY

Ever since the late nineteenth century psychologists have been questioning the value of play and subjecting it to classification. Piaget has come forward with a very simple classification. It is based on the three major ways in which we play, according to the sequence in which they first appear.

Because, for Piaget, all our activities are learning situations (whatever material and physical purposes they also serve) it follows that predominating play patterns must run parallel with the major periods of intellectual growth. As usual one must remember that as we grow we do not discard our earlier ways of learning but accumulate them: similarly, as we grow, we accumulate all our ways of playing too.

Piaget recognizes three main classes of play according to their sequence of appearance: they are practice games, symbolic games and games with rules. A fourth possible class could be constructional games, which emerge as an outgrowth of both symbolic and rule-controlled games and so cannot be put into the time sequence. Constructional games contain a considerable element of work as well as of play.

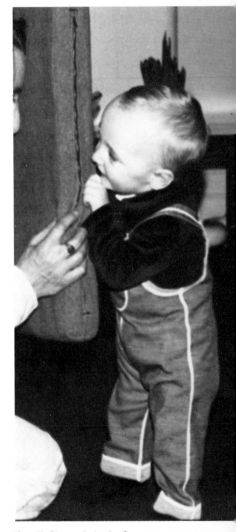

1 Evolution of practice games:

Practice games begin early in babyhood. We have already noticed a baby exploring his environment through play.

We could start by looking back to the second sub-period of babyhood with the baby 'sucking for sucking's sake'. Then, during the next sub-period, we might recall the kicking game to keep a dangling toy in motion. Certainly these, so often repeated, are practice games and we saw that satisfaction and learning stemmed from them.

It is in the fourth and fifth sub-periods of babyhood that study within play becomes more significant, yet not so dominant as to counterbalance the superabundance of play. Imitation is important too, especially if it offers a chance of communication with an adult. As an example, take the enthusiastic continuation of the game of waving 'good-bye', first precipitated by imitation. It becomes so enjoyable that it may frequently be put into action as soon as a visitor arrives. Or take 'Small', playing 'peekaboo' with his mother. It would be difficult to decide whether imitation or play predominated.

'Small'. Play or imitation?

Claire Denyse. A practice game with water.

In the last two babyhood sub-periods we find it even harder to distinguish whether enjoyable experiences are practice play or work. The child's shouts of delight, or perhaps his final smile, may show us that enjoyment predominates: serious contentment may mark the activity as pleasant mental work.

As a final example of practice games in late babyhood, let us look at Derek, with peals of laughter, running through a pool of water for the joy of creating a splash. He practised this game dozens of times one afternoon, occasionally deviating by jumping in an experimental way for the sake of study, but always returning to the simple run-through which must have given him the most pleasurable splash-feeling to assimilate into himself.

For Claire Denyse, at just over two, water play had become a practice game. Her interest in its properties became riveted and she would play for an hour or more. At each session practice play gradually gave way to intense active study.

Before we leave practice games we must stress one fact: practice games continue prolif\cly throughout childhood and less prolifically throughout our lives. What is skating or the Fosbury high-jump but a practice game of junior or adolescent life? If you see an 'executive' toy can you resist activating it time after time? Or do you dive from the edge of the pool dozens of times in one afternoon for the sheer joy of the experience? All these things, at whatever your age, are pure health-giving practice play.

The Fosbury high-jump.

2 Evolution of symbolic games:

Symbolism, symbolic play, symbolic games are so interconnected in babyhood and throughout toddlerhood and infancy that we can study them here as one.

Symbolic play evolves gradually over a long period of time. For ease we can look at four clear stages in its growth:

(a) First comes the symbolizing that we have already noticed well before the climax of babyhood. (b) Then in babyhood's sixth sub-period and well into toddlerhood the child enjoys a period of very simple 'make-believe'. (c) This merges into more complicated 'make-believe' just before the age of three. (d) Soon after he is four, and is ready for short spells of socializing with a few other children, he is seized by a desire to symbolize *exactly* any interesting happenings that he has witnessed: one could perhaps see this as the beginning of child drama. We must start by glancing back at examples recorded earlier in the book.

(a) Impulsive symbolizing and imitating in babyhood:

In the first chapter we saw a baby of a few weeks old impulsively symbolizing sucking and, soon after that, symbolizing the rhythm of his mother's speech by his own waving arm movements. In the fourth babyhood sub-period he displayed a happy re-enactment of his own well-known actions by pretending to eat or to sleep.

When, in the fifth sub-period, his spiral patterns of learning take on an element of experimentation, he often ritualizes the outcome of his

experiments. We have a picture here of Derek experimenting, not quite for the first time, with using a felt pen. First he enjoyed the smooth movement of the pen. Then he discovered the excitement of making scores of staccato dots. He looked at them with pride, then left the table and proceeded to jump up and down as if symbolically making more dots.

Many people who have never heard of Piaget will, nevertheless, know the classic story of his daughter[2] failing to open a matchbox and, in her efforts, repeatedly opening and closing her mouth as if in magic command. One only appreciates the full wonder of this story when one considers that the child had never seen her own mouth. We come back once more to Derek[3] gnashing his teeth! Both children were subconsciously expressing their wishes in symbolic language, for they had not yet acquired the tool of speech. Even so, since they were unconscious of their symbolizing, speech would have been useless. Whether they were symbolically talking to and commanding the toy itself or whether they were communicating to themselves about a new (if unsatisfactory) means to an end, each was symbolizing a possible new approach to the problem of the moment. At this age 'play', according to Piaget, 'begins to involve the "as if"'.[4]

Derek rising to symbolize dots.

(b) Symbolic play, early 'make-believe':

'Make-believe', from its very beginning, is *conscious*, playful symbolization. How many little girls of two years old have you watched pretend to sweep the kitchen floor in symbolic imitation of their mothers' actions? No brush is needed for the purpose: any object, or yet no object at all, would do. How many have you watched put dolls to sleep or give them jam to eat? A leaf or a piece of paper would serve as a spoon. How often have you seen such a child carry out, by 'delayed imitation', your own actions of the previous day? If you were driving the family car he can perfectly happily drive an upturned kitchen chair or any old box. He needs no car nor rapid movement to satisfy him as he symbolizes your actions in his play. Such play is a sign to you that he is beginning to form preconcepts and images of experiences that he has observed but has never had himself. He feels an urge to study them and, in their absence, symbolizing is his only possible way of doing so, 'Symbolic play is merely egocentric thought in its pure state'[5] and is still prelogical.

Sometimes symbolizing at this stage can be calm and quite still, as it was in the case of Peter and Louise at the end of a play-group session, sitting quietly in a box and pretending to be their mothers 'waiting in the car'. They continued to sit in great dignity even when Neil came and boisterously dragged them away.

Such imitative activities respond not only to a young toddler's urge to symbolize, but also depend on a feat of memory. The child must remember *your* activities. It is more difficult than remembering his own. There is an appropriate preconcept dawning in him and by his conscious symbolizing

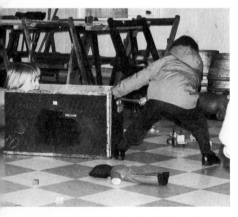

Peter and Claire Louise. Early make-believe.

[2] Jean Piaget, *The Origin of Intelligence*, pp. 337–38.
[3] See above, Chapter Four, p. 49.
[4] Jean Piaget, *The Origin of Intelligence*, p. 355.
[5] Jean Piaget, *Play, Dreams and Imitation in Childhood*, p. 166.

Claire Louise. Later make-believe.

of it he is feeding its growth. Yet this symbolic 'make-believe' is spontaneous in that he does it from an inner urge to play. The imaginativeness perhaps reaches its peak in such games as solo 'hide-and-seek'.

All these games are what Piaget calls an 'ego-study', in which the child is testing his own mastery over his environment.

(c) Symbolic play, later make-believe:

Like any other tool of intellectual development, 'make-believe' continues to expand until such time as it has served its purpose. Halfway through toddlerhood a child's preconcepts become firmly founded and his make-believe hankers to be anchored to reality too. No longer will isolated symbolic activities satisfy him. He now needs to symbolize activities in their total setting. The inverted kitchen chair (or car) now needs a garage, traffic lights and perhaps a white line. The gap between kitchen cabinets, the vacuum cleaner and a stick of celery will serve these three purposes well. You notice that he is beginning to use 'props' that have some slight similarity to the objects that they signify.

The prettiest example I have seen was Claire Louise sitting alone in a large garden to make a telephone call, with one daffodil trumpet to her ear and another to her mouth. Certainly she was symbolizing a known activity, but her action was triggered off by the shape of the daffodil cups. In Chapter Seven we introduced preconcepts as a 'jumble of ideas' that need to be integrated. In one telephone call Claire Louise was serving two of these converging streams of thought: we might add a third, for she was most certainly practising speech.

Many a child at this stage of symbolic play will symbolize the actions of his mother or his dog or kitten in an attempt to experience the feelings of that other being. It is interesting for the observer to decide whether it is symbolic play or imitation that predominates. If play predominates, the child is expressing himself *to* himself and merely using imitations as the means to that end: if imitation predominates he is studying his mother's or his pet's way of behaving. It is when he stresses both equally that his total learning from the experience is at its peak: it could be seen as a pleasant mental form of work.

The most gloriously extravagant example of the involvement of imitation in symbolic play that I have recorded was provided by Derek, at three and a half years old, who had been curled up beside his mother watching a symphony concert on television. Possibly, for him, the conductor seemed to be producing music with his wand. At the end of the concert Derek, without explanation, issued the five other people in the room with objects seemingly chosen at random (a pencil, a book, a teddy bear, a toy duck and a ball). He climbed on to a stool and, commanding us to 'play', conducted us vigorously and sang lustily as he did so. He was obviously convincing himself that music could be made by such arm-waving. He was not only imitating the conductor: he was identifying with him and assimilating the experience into his own preconcepts.

Shortly after Derek gave us this entertainment, Sir John Barbirolli said in a broadcast that in toddlerhood he had been accustomed to 'conducting' in his mother's drawing-room. He had always worn white gloves for the purpose and had been sure that the gloves were essential to production of the music.

(d) Symbolic play or child drama?

The stage before this will not have lasted long. Soon after the toddler is about four years old wear and tear on the inverted kitchen chair decreases and daffodils have a safer life in the garden. The child now begins to realize that he is pretending, and consequently needs more exact props as the tools for his pretences. He begins to project himself into inanimate objects. He makes them play *for* him, which is an exact reversal of his mimicking them. This may be catharsis, but more often it is not.

The small boy, feeling abandoned the moment his mother deposits him in a nursery school to go shopping, jumps on the nearest tricycle and rides it furiously to make it take him shopping too. He may well be instructing the tricycle to catch up with her, irrespective of the direction in which he is guiding it: if so, that is catharsis.

One could read many a hypothetical story into the picture of Agatha in her nursing uniform, but neither she nor her companion spoke throughout the game so no one could tell whether hers was catharsis or pure symbolic play. Her couch and stethoscope were very realistic toys.

It was no catharsis for four-year-old Stephen, who loved his weekly ten minutes in Quaker meeting. One Sunday he calmly roused himself from his quiet contentment, looked around at bent heads and announced clearly, 'My Teddy's gone to sleep too.' He patted Teddy gently. He had

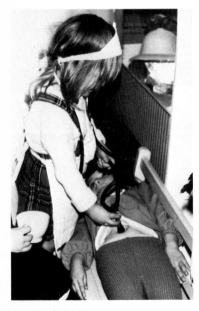

Agatha. Child drama.

Jessica sharing ideas with Emu.

been projecting his ideas into his toy and was content that it shared his pleasure.

Jessica was definitely sharing her delight with her puppet, Emu, as she talked to him of the darting fish she could see in the pool. Sharing ideas with one's toys is a typical feature of pure symbolic play. Until then Jessica had needed to absorb her toys and their potentials into herself: now she could project herself into her toys. Meanwhile, Claire Helen was absorbed in studying the fish and the hovering insects.

Catharsis or not, each of these is an example of a child symbolizing in play feelings which he believes he has projected into his toy, because they have overflowed in himself. It helps him to sort out the tangle in some of his preconcepts.

So by the end of toddlerhood a child, with the help of symbolic play, brings himself to terms with much in the world around him. Such symbolic play will continue throughout the intuitive period and then will gradually evolve into spontaneous drama. For many of us the tendency to 'make-believe' never dies.

3 Evolution of games with rules:

Rules, in themselves, bring to mind relationships between individuals. This means emphatically that a toddler, whose thoughts are still predominantly egocentric, can have no understanding of the essence of rules or true appreciation of them. Yet he can be trained to obey simple rules as, for example, in back-garden cricket or baseball. That implies that further discussion of games with rules has no firm place in this book and should be left to a later volume. Nevertheless, for the sake of tidyness and to round off a chapter on the intellectual value of play, it will be dealt with briefly here. For all that has preceded it in this chapter has been a necessary laying of foundations for games with rules and, indeed, for a healthy attitude in life towards rules in general.

Most children of less than about seven years old have little desire for rules in their play: even if they accept the idea of using them they apply them inaccurately and half-heartedly, for rules do not seem appropriate to the spirit of play. Infant children can accept rules as a form of compulsion from adults. Hand-washing before meals and care in crossing the road are excellent examples of rules that can become habits even in toddlerhood days. But habits are *not play*. Such rules may enter cathartic play, but otherwise they have no play value.

It is only perhaps at about the age of seven that a child becomes sufficiently interested in other people's *thoughts* for him to pay attention to enjoying rules. Up to this point he has shown interest in other people only for their tangible, practical qualities. He has cared whether they are pretty, helpful, intolerant, well dressed, kind or a nuisance to him. He may have been jealous of some of them. But he has not wondered about their points of view.

In the intuitive period, he socializes spontaneously with others of his age. By the onset of junior life he normally becomes an active member of 'gangs' of his peers. With true gang-psychology he becomes interested in the thinking and in the needs of gang members. Thus, gradually, he examines the fairness or unfairness of specific competitive games. Equally gradually he comes to recognize that those abstract impositions called rules are the yardstick of fairness which can influence the enjoyment of a game. So he even takes an interest in the rules themselves. Frequently gangs become so obsessed by the whole idea of rules that they spend more time in breaking off from play to invent new rules than in actually getting on with the game.

This runs parallel to a junior's desire to reason about practical situations. What better material things could he have to hold his reasoning steady than bats and balls and gangs of 'cops and robbers'? He may learn the rules of games from his father: the members of his gang make the rules of 'cops and robbers' for themselves. Both these types of rules in play are of great value in the child's development of character, but it is through the second type that we can most easily examine his thinking.

The rules of marbles:

Piaget had the inspiration of probing children's responses to the rules of marbles. He reasoned that the rules must be child-influenced rather than adult-given because adults rarely remember the exact rules by which they once played.

Piaget found that those in the intuitive period could neither understand nor obey the rules of the game although they were convinced that they could do both. Like the toddlers they soon drifted back to using marbles for symbolic or practice play. They were not spontaneously interested in competition and, therefore, not in fairness, and so not in rules. Like Alice in Wonderland they thought, 'Everyone can win.'

But juniors, as we saw earlier (page 90), are social animals, spontaneously interested in one another's *ideas*. So their play becomes social. Rules become interesting as laws, accepted by mutual consent, to suit the spirit of the game. One should either obey them or agree to adapt them. So far so good! They take joy in concocting innumerable and complicated rules. But it is well into this period of truly valuing rules before juniors really trouble to learn the rules by which they think they are playing. So confusion can ensue.

For the benefit of my students, I frequently interrupted children playing marbles in front of closed-circuit television cameras and asked them to teach me the rules. Juniors, surprised at questions about where rules came from, made such suggestions as that 'they were made in a factory' or 'made by my great-grandfather'. The richest example of confusion was recorded in detail and can be abbreviated to the following:

'Do you play football' 'Yes.' 'Are there rules in football too?' 'Yes. Lots!' 'Can you tell me some?' Intermingled statements came forth, some of which were the rules of the game, more were the ways of keeping score or of 'being sent off' or 'having one's name took'. A few were rules of betting. By general agreement a few specific rules (such as 'offside', 'barging', and goalkeeper's privileges) were chosen from a game played between league teams on the previous Saturday. 'Were those rules very important to the game?' 'Yes. Of course!' 'Why?' 'To make it fair.' 'Who made those rules?' 'The captains of the teams.' 'Together?' 'No. Each captain with his manager.' Then, after some argument among the children themselves, a final clear statement. 'The captain of Preston made them for Preston and the captain of United made them for United.' 'Are you really sure about that?' After a long pause and from a very thoughtful boy, 'No. For Manchester United it would be Georgie Best.' (He was referring, of course, to the most popular soccer player of the day.)

CONCLUSION

Play, merging into sport as childhood develops, has for a long time been recognized as one of the greatest character-builders in life. In the past this influence was generally considered to be almost entirely due to its effect on healthy physical growth. That influence and value should never be *under*estimated. But physical and mental exercises necessarily integrate themselves. The thinking that takes place in play is of enormous value to learning because it is assimilated at a time of pleasurable experience. Furthermore it is predominantly through one's thinking about such real situations that one sets out one's considered ideas on justice, reward and retribution.

Specific ideas cannot give way to generalized analysis until the abstract thinking of adolescence takes over from childhood's random concrete examples. Then experiences, gleaned from respect for the rules in sport (experienced at the moment or culled from the child's past), act as one's reference grid for all sorts of philosophical meditation about altruism, justice, equity and, ultimately, about law.

That could be the theme of a whole book. Play, imitation, work, speech, moral judgment, physical and mental growth are all interlocked and dependent on one another, and the nurturing of each individually increases the development of them all.

FOR THE MORE SERIOUS STUDENT
PLAY AND IMITATION

1 Piaget sees:

(i) Play as excess of assimilation over accommodation.

(ii) Imitation as excess of accommodation over assimilation.

(iii) Maximum learning as resulting from equilibrium between the two. For details of greater niceties one should examine the diagram in Piaget's *Play, Dreams and Imitation* (Introduction). A student who wants to take this study further will find many examples in that book and in his *Moral Judgement in the Child*.

2 Further technical terms include:

(i) 'Vocal contagion'. A baby as young as twenty days may sometimes imitate the tone of his mother's voice.

(ii) 'Mental combinations' are the outcome of schemas becoming independent of immediate perception.

(iii) Piaget would use the terms 'signal' or 'index' to denote a movement (such as biting one's lip) made by an adult to invite a child to do the same. Such a movement might be studied and copied by the time the child is about eight months old. Briefly, a 'signal' stimulates an activity. It comes from someone or something other than the child and sets a known schema into action spontaneously. In contrast, the older child himself creates 'symbols' which refer to known activities and stimulate in him further thoughts about them. Piaget makes much of signs, indices and symbols. This will be enlarged upon in Chapter Ten.

3 Piaget considers that imitation depends partly on the child's estimate of the person he imitates. 'From two to seven representative imitation develops spontaneously, often being unconscious because of its ease and egocentrism, whereas at about seven or eight years old it becomes deliberate and takes its place in intelligence as a whole.'[6] Imitation is hyperadaptation. Play is a relaxation from adaptation and gives a 'feeling of virtuosity or power'.[7]

4 Piaget's theories, because they depend on the proportional relationship between knowing rules (or laws) and holding respect for them, would support the reaction of a normally law-abiding citizen who is also a

[6] Jean Piaget, *Play, Dreams and Imitation*, p. 72.
[7] *Play, Dreams and Imitation*, p. 89.

conscientious objector to a law that he sees as morally wrong. They would not support the activist who breaks laws just because he thinks they are unfair, especially if it is from his own (selfish) point of view.

5 Babyhood is a period of impulsive symbolism since 'the symbol has not yet been freed as an element of thought'.[8] It is *not* conscious symbolism: it is an internal quasi-imitation.

6 The recognition of common characteristics, as shown by Claire Louise (the daffodil cups and telephone), is one of the earliest foundations of logic.[9]

7 Nineteenth-century psychologists began to contradict the prevalent idea that play was a waste of energy. Karl Groos and Claparède saw two distinct values in play. They saw it as 'pre-exercise' like the play of a kitten practising with a ball for catching mice in the future. They also saw it as symbolic imagination. Stanley Hall and C.G. Jung associated it with heredity. They claimed that particular games follow each other at relatively constant age-stages which correspond to the history of man. There were others who saw play as infantile dynamics because of its impulsiveness and lack of coherence. For Freud all the past is preserved in the unconscious, so this must include storage of play experiences. Conversely Freud claimed that, by watching a child at play, one could unravel *what* he was putting into his unconscious for storage. Freud also saw the symbolism in play releasing a content that otherwise might be repressed (catharsis) in contrast to Groos's idea that symbolism was a striving for results not yet achieved.

Piaget was the first to evaluate scientifically the relationship of play to moral judgment.

[8] *Play, Dreams and Imitation*, p. 120.
[9] Jean Piaget, *The Early Growth of Logic.*

CHAPTER NINE

Thoughts That Evoke Language

Communication, speech, gesturing, writing, reading! To some extent these words are all synonyms for 'language', not meaning that they are identical but 'statements that may in some contexts or in some of their senses be substituted for one another without affecting their meaning' (*OED*). For all of us body language is as effective as speech. For the small child it tends to be the predominant way of expressing his thoughts. The early growth of language has already been touched upon in previous chapters since it is too closely intermingled with other development for its contribution to have been ignored.

The key point with regard to language, in Piaget's theory of learning, is that thought necessarily develops from babyhood onwards and is at first expressed by body language alone and then by symbolism and by symbolic play. Even the baby is often sufficiently excited by his discoveries to need to share them in this way. Vocal sounds that precede speech form part of such body language and these vocal sounds ultimately mature into speech. With this in mind the first part of this chapter and much of the next chapter will deal with the wider issue of language as a whole without confining it to speech, for even in toddlerhood gestures are still the predominant form of language.

No one could doubt, even from a photograph alone, that eighteen-month-old Joanne was asking to go out. When her request failed she took refuge in catharsis and carried out the mature spiral experiment of going into the snow in her father's shoes.

'SEMI-WORDS'

As babyhood draws to a close and gives way to toddlerhood the child feels a greater urge than ever before to communicate his growing preconceptual ideas to all around him. At the same time his vocal muscles, which he has been straining to use since his first day, become stronger and more controlled. His urge to imitate is expanding too. As he hears sounds connected with his experiences he practises imitating them. The sounds may be bird-song or dogs barking or the sound of traffic or of

Joanne. A wordless request.

Joanne. Experimental walking.

thunder: they may equally well be words or sentences spoken by adults. He symbolizes in sound all these exciting things that he hears. So 'semi-words' are formed and become a vocal language of his own.

The joy of communicating through speech has been born. It gives him such pleasure and such a feeling of power that by the time he reaches toddlerhood he chatters rather incoherently about all his equally incoherent thoughts.

We have all been subjected to the torrents of disconnected announcements that can burst forth as soon as a child feels confident of conveying his profound discoveries to others in this way. I can remember Nathan Isaacs speaking of 'the glorious help and disastrous hindrance of language'; he argued that many a child, soon after acquiring words, may get so carried away with the sensuous pleasure of hearing himself speak that he expends on meaningless chatter energy that might otherwise have gone into preconceptual thought. The child thus expresses his thoughts from preconcepts that are themselves vague. He often chatters ahead of his thoughts. Frequently he echoes other people's statements lucidly and meaninglessly, when he finds it too cumbersome to express his own.

Disastrous as it is, this chatter also helps him to fit the new tool, speech, into the over-all enjoyment of his environment.

As Dr Bronowski said in his television series, *The Ascent of Man*, 'No scientist could accept the idea that he is to make a discovery and then not to publish it.' I am sure Dr Bronowski would have included in that the child-discoverer, however young he might be.

This state of constant chatter can be charming in the two-year-old telling you tales from his egocentric point of view as he practises his new-found skill. Some of what he tells you may seem to be lies. He cannot, in fact, be lying, for as yet he can have no concept of truth and lies. He cannot invent ideas. His learning, to date, has been of completely straightforward facts and skills. He can imagine nothing else except perhaps frequently heard fictional stories. He can imagine re-experiencing what he has once enjoyed (for example, any parental kindness). Sublimated longings for repeats of such enjoyed experiences can register in his mind as if they were happening again. So he can misunderstand. And he can echo.

A sociable three-year-old girl was in a car in which a friend of mine was a guest. To make conversation, the child said, 'When I was a little girl I used to sing baritone.' What would have been your reaction? Was it a lie, an echo, a misunderstanding, a confused preconcept? Or just good social training in putting guests at their ease? It was all these things except the lie.

Toddlerhood is a period for laying down the habit of talkativeness which stays with most of us throughout our lives.[1] Gradually two major changes take place: the intellectual content of our talk improves as our intellect grows and most of us learn how and when to talk less. One wonders whether the adult who talks on, egocentrically and mean-inglessly, boring us with clichés, is to be rejected or sympathized with; his childish chatter stems from the fact that society has not helped him to enrich his thinking far beyond the preconceptual stage. So, according to Piaget, speech is the outcome of thought at all ages.

GROWTH OF THE TECHNICAL SKILL OF SPEECH

Earlier in this book mention was made of *vocal* communications that preceded speech, such as Amber's unsuccessful attempt to exercise her vocal cords.[2] Later on, sucking, licking and chewing strengthen control of the mouth and throat muscles as well as serving their obvious purposes. We saw Amber again, at four months old, having gained sufficient control to blow large bubbles (in attempted speech) and to tune in to the lilt of her mother's conversation (see p. 38).

It is at about this time that babies who are often talked to seem to begin to respond to the tune of specific phrases and to practise them. This tells us clearly that they are listening to our speech and attempting to learn from it. They are grasping the sound patterns they hear without noticing the details of words within those patterns.

[1] Professor Noam Chomsky, the great linguist and philosopher, claims that language is inherently programmed to grow in the human race.
[2] See Chapters One and Three, pp. 25 and 28.

Then, during the fifth sub-period of babyhood, the child learns to associate words with their meanings. He cannot at first reproduce those words: he still expresses himself by gestures. Quite early in the period he will respond correctly to 'Come Here!', or 'Bring Daddy his shoes!'

In the next few months he will build up a supply of words with which to express himself, always with supportive gestures. Joanne, at about twenty months old, had been 'helping' her grandfather who was using beautifully rectangular, doormat-shaped turfs to lay a new lawn. That evening she spread several newspapers on the sitting-room floor and stamped heavily on them saying, 'G'anddad! Mats!'

In the next few months the child gains a surprising agility to express himself in phrases. We know he is listening to full sentences, for he soon pours forth sentences that are grammatically constructed. By some peculiar preconceptual leap he has acquired an ear for regular plurals, regular past tenses, verbs with their nouns and adjectives correctly scattered, and all with meaningful intonation.

From this point the young toddler bombards us with torrents of speech, freely littered with meaningful new words such as 'sheeps' and 'mans' and things that are 'importanter' than others. He is gaining the skills of speech faster than exact vocabulary. It is all a further example of interacting dynamically with his environment rather than depending on being taught. It highlights the fact that language is the tool of his thoughts rather than the master of them. Yet he also likes being taught by being talked to.

We have leapt ahead rather fast instead of dwelling sufficiently on the stage of 'semi-words' and distorted words. It is with them that the observer can most easily trace the strong bond that a word has with its related preconcept.

DISTORTED WORDS AND THEIR PRECONCEPTS

Perhaps the distorted word is a step nearer adult speech than is the semi-word. This can be illustrated by Peter, who, at about two and a half years old, called a noisy group of adults to silence by shouting 'Peking! Peking!'. His ears, sharper than ours, had heard the telephone ringing in the adjoining room. We realized the connection only when his mother picked up the receiver and, after a second's pause, said 'Speaking!' For us, Peter's word must have had an attractive ring about it, for we all called the telephone 'Peking' for several days after that.

At about the same age Peter had his first taste of strawberries, and took a great liking to them. At every meal he asked for 'Chorbellies'. Gradually he applied the word to all kinds of soft fruit. At his easel he prodded great blobs of red paint on to paper as he chanted the expressive word.

Peter had reached the stage of listening fairly intently to words. His slight inaccuracies were more to do with the vagueness of detail in all his preconcepts than with an inability to hear. We know his hearing was good, if only because of the tale of the telephone.

Like Peter, Derek at the same age brought something of the flavour of his experiences into distorting an adult's word. He and his father had been playing football against a brick wall, creating a thudding sound. Derek called it 'fooboar' in rhythm with the thuds. Next day he challenged me to a game of 'fooboar' and produced for the purpose a small ball and a cricket bat. Confused preconcepts again! Over the next few weeks 'fooboar' was used to denote all ball games, ninepins, snap, 'I Spy', dancing and a modified game of snakes and ladders. Derek was too young to classify and sub-classify [3] games, but he had gleaned a general idea of games in the way of a preconcept and accepted the idea with sufficient enthusiasm to know how to express it in words. So he brought both prelogic and music into his language.

One must wonder to what extent it is wise to lead the child away from semi-words, distorted words and incorrect plurals and past tenses. Or should one even, perhaps, echo his childish talk?

If baby-talk is the child's own invented word bursting forth straight from his vibrant preconcept, I would join in enthusiastically and use it with him at the time. Correct words are important but the skill of thinking and then communicating is more important still. I would never dampen enthusiasm. Acceptance of anything a child says buttresses his growing confidence in speaking. Anyone can help by extending the conversation, using more conventional words that are within his understanding, for one must help the preconcepts to expand if one wishes the vocabulary to do so.

Echoing his own semi-words is different from teaching him such words as 'pussy' or 'armoos': he can just as easily learn 'cat' or 'cows'. It is not the technical acquisition of words that a toddler finds difficult, however complicated those words are, but the ideas to which they apply. To take an example, snow is almost impossible to imagine if you have never experienced it, so most English toddlers find the word 'snow' hard to learn except in the occasional year when they get a chance to play with it; in contrast, 'television' is a complex but meaningful word, easily learned.

This last example leads one to remember that toddlers today share in many rich experiences with television programmes and, so long as they really *are* meaningful, gain vocabulary from them as well as from their human contacts. It is sometimes revealing to learn what unexpected programmes can interest so young a child. Derek joined in a conversation about the possibility of rain when a picnic was under discussion. 'It will be sun,' he said firmly. 'How do you know?' 'George Luce said so.' 'Who is George Luce?' 'The man who gives us weather.' And *this* from a four-year-old! From the point of view of meaningfulness the promise of sun means much to a child brought up in rainy Lancashire, especially to one who had been half-promised a picnic for the next day. It is even strong enough to help him to concentrate on the speech of a conventional weather forecaster. As for his preconcept of the science of weather systems, the less said the better! He really only had the choice between magic and an all-powerful George Luce. Yet Derek had learned that it was 'done by isobars'.

---

[3] Jean Piaget and Bärbel Inhelder, *The Early Growth of Logic in the Child*, Chapter 5.

CONFUSION CAUSED BY ABSTRACT WORDS

We have stressed that confused speech generally comes from confused preconcepts. Sometimes it comes from an inability to grasp in clear-cut fashion the meanings of words that are abstract, even if frequently used. I experienced an example of this after taking the photograph of Sarah in Chapter Six. The story shows how linguistic skills and structures can be stronger than an understanding of the vocabulary used.

Sarah was staying with her grandmother, who had just given her a lemon-coloured drink. The following conversation began.

Grandmother to M.S., 'Do you want tea or coffee?'

M.S., 'Coffee, please!'

Sarah stretched towards a bottle of attractively coloured orange juice with, 'I want coffee. I want coffee!' much repeated.

Grandmother, 'Say "May I have . . . ?"'

Sarah, obediently, 'May I have? I want coffee.'

This went on for some time, then M.S., picking up the orange juice and thoughtlessly reinforcing the unfortunate word, 'Is this what you want?'

Sarah bounced happily as she stretched out both hands, 'No!' Her tone of voice belied the word.

M.S., offering Sarah her own coffee, 'What about this?'

Sarah, sadly shaking her head and again stretching for the orange juice, 'Yes! I want coffee.'

'Don't worry', said her grandmother, 'she always confuses "Yes" and "No".'

One might agree that a bit of gradual correction of this use of the English language could be wise. But Sarah got her message across and the *structure* of her sentences was correct.

PIAGET'S CLASSIFICATION OF SPEECH[4]

As is usual with Piaget, the classification runs parallel with the growth of intellectual periods and sub-periods. Piaget sees only two main categories of speech, 'egocentric speech' and 'socialized speech', which emerge in that order as the toddler's whole way of life slips gradually from the egocentric towards the social. Each category can be subdivided into more particular speech forms and, as usual, all the earlier forms stay with us, gradually decreasing in emphasis, throughout life.

1 EGOCENTRIC SPEECH:

Egocentric speech starts with 'echolalia' which is quickly followed by 'monologue' and then by 'collective monologue'. All of these then intermingle until the end of toddlerhood in proportions that vary according to the child's own emotional security.

(a) Echolalia:
As the word suggests, echolalia is the child's own echoing of speech that

---

[4] Jean Piaget, *The Language and Thought of the Child*, general theme.

Janet Ann and Julian. Echolalia.

he has heard. It has the further implication that he is echoing only the sound and not the meaning: hence it is only slightly motivated by preconceptual learning.

The simplest example I can offer is of Derek, at the time of a Welsh eisteddfod,[5] going around the house for days on end chanting, 'Llangollen! Llangollen!' He was not Welsh. He had no idea of the meaning but he took sensuous delight in its broadcast sound. Joanne took joy in chanting a distorted version of a word overheard. Her version was 'splitzophenic'.

Most examples are more complex and are tied in with an element of monologue, as in the following episode.

In a nursery school four-year-old Janet Anne was painting a house and burst into monologue, saying to no one in particular, 'I'm painting my house.' Julian, standing at the easel beside her and concentrating fixedly on his own painting of his father said, 'I'm painting *my* house.' It was a meaningless echo. Neither was interested in the other's painting nor in the other's speech. As Piaget might have said, 'words thrown out were caught on the bounce like balls'.[6] Julian and Janet Anne were accepting one another just as casually and absent-mindedly as 'Small' (in Chapter Five) first accepted the puppy, Sheenah. Their thoughts were elsewhere. Janet Anne was speaking in monologue and Julian's words were echolalia.

[5] Held at Llangollen.
[6] Jean Piaget, *The Language and Thought of the Child*, p. 13.

(b) Monologue:

We have already recorded (in Chapter Seven) Beth's soliloquy as she sat alone in the back of a car. She felt contented that we were near her in the front seats so she was happy to talk to herself: she had no idea that we were listening.

Similarly you may have heard such a monologue from your toddler talking to himself or to his toys as you work in the next room. Occasionally he will toddle through to make sure that you are still there, yet he gives no thought to the fact that you might be listening. He still returns to describe to himself the path that his toy train is taking or to instructing it to go through a tunnel.

These monologues serve an essential stage in children's learning to speak.

(c) Collective monologue:

In previous chapters we have spoken of 'parallel play', and it is during parallel play that collective monologue is most frequently heard. Parallel play is prevalent at birthday parties or in play groups where interesting toys are plentiful.

A few weeks ago I watched half a dozen four-year-olds rush joyfully at a wheelbarrow and push it along at a running pace for a considerable time, sometimes wordlessly or with unintelligible squeals, but sometimes shouting about the barrow. No shout was replied to other than in echolalia. Each child only considered vaguely that another might be listening, but none ever made any effort to check this nor expected any reply. So far, it was collective monologue. Social interest started only when one child jumped on to the barrow. Then response to commands *was* expected but it was not forthcoming except in the sense that a fight ensued.

All the shouting had been collective monologue in which the subject of common interest (pushing the barrow) masked from the observer the fact that it was not socialized speech. No child there was interested in any other child's *thoughts*, only in his possessions or his actions. So none would have been able to extend in speech the subject-matter introduced by another except to argue, mostly in negatives, about an immediate incident. That is why such arguments so soon give way to physical tussles.

If, however, an adult had intervened with conversation, before the fight, the result might have been very different, as shown by the next example. It involves extracts from a collective monologue in progress while the accompanying pictures were taken.

Jane, in the first picture, murmured, 'My Mum's in our house. She's comin' to get me soon.' (She was unaware that it was still morning and that she had the afternoon ahead before 'Mum' came.) As Emma joined her at the next easel Jane gazed past her into the room and then continued her painting and her monologue. Emma started on a monologue about painting a pink house. Jane echoed about her own pink house (which was, in fact, purple) and then an adult joined in. 'What a pretty picture, Jane. What is it?' 'It's my Mum,' said Jane, brightening to a smile. No

Jane. Monologue.

longer was she feeling nostalgic nor relying on monologue. She was communicating. Further remarks brought a flow of explanation. 'There's my Mum coming and the sun's shining on it (the house) and there she's lit a fire (outside the house) and there's smoke from the chimney.' This was undoubtedly socialized speech, spoken for the sake of communicating and full of what Piaget classes as 'adapted information'. It *extended* the thoughts submitted by the adult.

Part of the conversation revealed that Jane was not all sure whether she had had her school dinner that day: for such a child measurement of time is very vague. The social conversation would have continued for as long as the adult was prepared to stay.

Jane was removed from the easel and Gillian took over, starting a picture and a soliloquy on 'Dad'. Meanwhile Emma went on painting, sometimes silently and occasionally murmuring her thoughts. Neither child was listening to, as contrasted to hearing, the other. Each was contentedly practising speech. Probably each concluded that she was interesting the other, but she did not check upon the fact.

2 SOCIALIZED SPEECH:

Socialized speech comes through socialization of thought and so, as has been illustrated, comes first through conversation with adults, for it is with them that a toddler socializes most easily. From adults he expects replies to questions just as he himself expects to answer adults' questions. And he extends any line of thought with 'adapted information'.

Jane and Emma. Collective monologue.

Jane to an adult. Socialized speech.

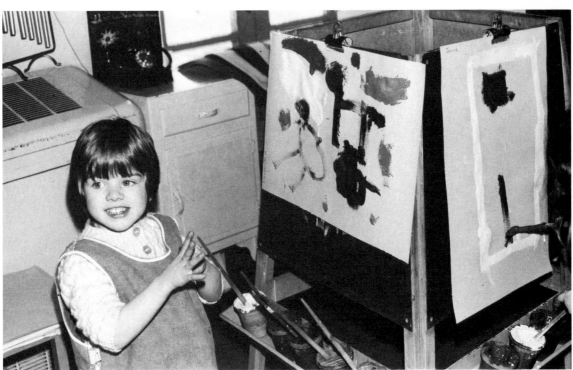

Karen. Criticism or threat?

Within a community of toddlers adapted information is rare. One can, of course, train even a small child to welcome child visitors, to thank them for presents or to other such social courtesies. A toddler very rarely extends spontaneously a line of thought expressed by another toddler.

Piaget and others have found that the socialized speech of toddlerhood tends to be predominantly criticism, commands, requests, threats, and appeals. Just one photograph will suffice for this. It is of Karen. Whether she is expressing criticism or a threat is not certain, but it is fairly clear from her expression that it is one or the other. There can be no doubt that she was using socialized speech rather than monologue. The message was certainly intended to register!

To use one more quotation, 'The child does not, in the first instance, communicate with his fellow beings in order to share thoughts and reflections. He does so in order to play.'[7] He cannot share his insubstantial preconcepts with others whose thinking is equally nebulous. Yet, as we have seen from all the examples so far in this book, a toddler's conversation with adults can be communicative and sharing. Toddlers see an adult as omniscient, and this faith in him steadies their own thoughts. Through such conversations they build up the skills of speech as well as enlarging their own horizons. Both the skills and the enriched preconcepts will be of inestimable value once these children begin to form fully fledged concepts during early school life.

It is at about the age of six that a great leap forward in socialized speech generally takes place. Then, suddenly, a child 'cannot keep a single

[7] *The Language and Thought of the Child*, p. 27.

thought secret'.[8] He chatters interminably, generally concentrating his efforts upon one transitory 'best friend'. His chatter has a conversational trend, for he now has the intellectual ability to be interested in the thoughts as well as the actions of his peers. He contrives to interest the other child with factual information. But that takes us beyond the limits of this book, so it is another story.

FOR THE MORE SERIOUS STUDENT
LANGUAGE AND THOUGHT

Points to concentrate on are:

1 A child needs to have ideas to talk about before he can have a desire to talk. Talk may be in body language, in art or in speech. As adults we too use all such forms.

2 Vocal efforts to speak start as soon as ever a mother holds a conversation with her child. The child strives for voice-control right through babyhood. Then comes rhythmic tuning-in, followed by semi-words, distorted words, words that imply sentences, phrases that imply sentences and then sentences. Quite often a one-year-old child will use nouns as verbs. He will confuse abstract words such as 'yes' and 'no' or 'in' and 'out'.

3 Egocentric speech includes echolalia, monologue and collective monologue. A child tends to start conversations with such words as 'He' and 'She', assuming, egocentrically, that the listener knows who and what he is talking about. This is one of the many examples of preconceptual confusion in preconceptual speech.

4 Socialized speech between child and parent can start as early as fourteen months. Before the age of two he is asking plenty of 'What's that?' questions which show that he has grasped the significance of words. By the time he is two and a half he asks innumerable questions, but rarely involving 'Why?', because he has no idea of reasoning. Similarly he rarely uses the word 'because' correctly, and arguments become a 'clash of affirmations'.[9] By the age of three his structure of language is fairly good. Between three and eight years old he will acquire a vocabulary of five thousand words or more.

5 Girls seem to acquire words before boys.

6 Socialized speech within groups of preconceptual children is rare except for commands, requests and threats, though collective monologue can be mistaken for social speech.

7 Full socialized speech contains commands, requests, threats, questions, answers, criticisms and adapted information.

8 Parents can best help a child to develop speech by helping him to develop his curiosity so that he has ideas to speak about. Such experience

[8] *The Language and Thought of the Child*, p. 41.
[9] *The Language and Thought of the Child*, p. 23.

helps him to reinforce his actions with words. Frequent conversations help him to structure his sentences.

9 Serious students would do well to read good, observant, philosophical literature about preconceptual children, such as the very simple poems by A.A. Milne (e.g. Christopher Robin, of his dormouse, 'I think, I think I will call him Jim *'cos* I am so fond of him').[10] (See 4 above.)

10 Piaget sees soliloquizing as 'interior' language resulting from monologues. Preconceptual children do a lot of 'romancing' and believe in magic.

11 So language evolves from the growth of mental images and of thought patterns, and throughout the preconceptual period body language, often accompanying speech, is stronger than speech, although speech becomes plentiful.

12 Professor Chomsky's thesis that language is pre-programmed in us all fits in well with Piaget's view that all human learning and intellectual achievement have a biological basis. Chomsky would claim that natural selection of the fittest has stabilized language so that it is inherited by us all, for there is a set of principles common to all languages. He would contrast language with the number concept (which is also a mental attribute common to all humans) for one cannot see any reason why mathematics should ensure natural selection of the fittest: hypothesizing beyond all evidence can surely not be a selective tool! The same argument would apply to those with scientific capacities for creating *new* scientific thoughts hypothetically, beyond any evidence.

[10] A.A. Milne, *When We Were Very Young*, p. 5.

CHAPTER TEN

The Road to Writing and Reading

It is generally during toddlerhood that a child first discovers that making marks on paper is a further way of expressing his nebulous thoughts. That will apply more particularly to the toddler who has frequently seen his parents writing and who is accustomed to having stories read to him while he 'reads' the pictures on the opposite page. He may have experimented during babyhood in the mechanical, sensuous experience of scribbling with crayons or pencils: now he scribbles for the added purpose of communicating the preconceptual ideas that are brewing in him. And he will probably chatter about these ideas as he scribbles. In the last chapter we looked at this from the point of view of speech: now let us look at it as it affects the roots of writing.

It matters little to the child whether adults call his efforts 'writing' or 'pictures', for he sees no difference between such terms. What does matter to him is that he has discovered another outlet for his ideas, another way of stating them, to add to (and to entangle with) his bodily gestures, his imitation, his speech and his musical efforts.

The sheer scribble that comes first is pure symbolic gesture and exploration of technique.

The distorted pictures that follow are the child's first recognizable achievements. If we study them imaginatively and with our own knowledge of his psychology in mind, we shall find that they reveal to us an imbalance in his visual discrimination. He is selective of features that are most meaningful to him in people or in things. For example, his mother's face means more to him than the whole of the rest of her, so he draws it disproportionately big.

Towards the middle or end of toddlerhood an interest in aesthetically pleasing shapes begins to dawn. That must be dealt with much more fully later in this chapter and also in the chapter on pre-mathematics. Suffice it to say here that this is a point at which an interest in the shapes of letters can begin.

Piaget, at appropriate points throughout his work, pays particular attention to the content of children's pictures: he does not specifically single out writing, but its growth fits in with his general theme of a child's learning in toddlerhood and in the intuitive period.[1]

MESSAGES IN TODDLERHOOD ART

As this book proceeds, more and more of the subjects that we analyse have already been touched upon in another context. This emphasizes the fact that preconceptual development is conglomerate. That applies particularly to the contribution made by child art within the growth of the child's thought.

It must first be made clear that we are discussing only spontaneous art. There is no point in asking a child to paint a fire-engine (for you to analyse) if he, at that moment, is thinking of painting his puppy. He would have to abandon his thoughts for your thoughts and it is unlikely that the result would be either a vivid or compelling artistic statement. If, on the other hand, you leave him to paint his puppy the result, though distorted, may be full of puppyhood vigour. I believe Emerson once said, 'A vivid thought brings the power to paint it, and in proportion to the depth of its source is the force of its projection.' This would apply as much to the vivid work of a toddler as to that of Van Gogh.

If given a free range of paints and crayons, a toddler will be likely to do most pictures in bright, or even lurid, colours and absorb the sensuously satisfying effects into himself. Apart from that colour factor the content of typical examples of his work can easily be examined here in black and white reproductions.

(a) The earliest stage:

Jeremy (in Chapter Seven), drawing for us his puff of smoke, was just passing from pure scribble to expressing on paper what he had selected as the most interesting feature of a vibrant experience. Like an abstract expressionist he was the energy source: the forces of the paint were released in his picture.[2]

Then, in next to no time, he leapt from painting the abstract to painting his first recognizable pictures, although the force of abstract expressionism has always stayed with him.

James Alistair had also just taken that leap. He drew his mother, who was working beside him and occasionally talking to him. He did not see his mother with our eyes. He chose to see what he remembered most vividly, a large face with two eyes and a mouth above them, and then, when his mother spoke again, another, blacker open mouth beneath, with teeth showing. Unfortunately, at that point, Graeme asked, 'Where is her nose?' James Alistair put it in between the eyes and added, 'And *these* are the holes at the end.' Then came the finishing touches. Arms and legs sprouted from near the sides of the head and a small body was squeezed into a space at the bottom of the paper.

[1] His theories of intellectual growth later in life have also been applied to the teaching of illiterate adults as, for example, with the Gattegno coloured alphabet designed in the first place for a literacy drive in Ethiopia.
[2] See H.W. Janson and Samuel Cauman, *History of Art for Young People.*

James Alistair's mother's face.
('Synthetic incapacity.')

James Alistair had made his statement of what his mother meant to him. It did not matter to James Alistair how his mother's parts synthesized. Piaget calls this a stage of 'synthetic incapacity' in art. And that synthetic incapacity is in the child's whole thinking too.

There was such a synthetic incapacity in Paul Daniel's picture of 'Wuzzy' (Chapter Seven), with the numerous wheels unattached to the car and with the lack of proportion in the other cars, whether they were on the road or inverted in mid-air.

For years to come a degree of synthesis will be lacking in the child's art. That can be seen even in pictures of scenery drawn by juniors, where a streak of vivid blue sky is often separated from the landscape by a 'no-man's land' of blank paper.

(b) A later stage of toddlerhood art:

With the acquisition of some synthesis in mid-toddlerhood there comes a gradual recognition of shape. Limbs and body may be joined to the head of a person. Before long, they will all join in the correct places but the proportions will continue to be wildly erratic.

We saw an example of this in Chapter Nine as Julian painted his father. Previously he had painted his mother too. The finished results of both show synthesis and shape.

His colours were obviously chosen for the joy of their effects. 'Daddy' was bright blue in outline, with purple eyes and mouth enclosed and in about the right positions. Around the right eye were two white and three red spots – 'Daddy's' thoughts, for all we know, or even food that 'Daddy' had eaten, for it is quite usual at this stage for a child to paint in something invisible that he knows to be there. 'Mummy' had a bright red outline, with blue hair and eyes and mouth. Her hands were a gentle pink.

Arms and legs joined securely. In the case of 'Daddy', the legs extended well into the face. Or could that bottom bit below the eyes be 'Daddy's'

Julian's 'Mummy' and 'Daddy'.
('Intellectual realism.')

body? If so, two of the red blobs could be his mouth. Both parents had arms with enormous, welcoming hands.

The interest in shape is there, even if not too well achieved. The eyes, which Julian has most often gazed at, are beautifully round and the limbs are straight.

But Julian's thoughts still dominate his pictures, overruling his consciousness of shapes. The eyes and mouth of both parents stand out from the rather large mass of human comfortableness that his parents stand for. Both parents are up in the air above him on things called legs. To a small child 'Daddy's' legs must seem infinitely long; that could be why they extend into his body.

In Chapter Eleven we shall refer to these pictures again with regard to topological features.

By the end of this stage of artistic development body, limbs and head come much more nearly into proportion, but the child becomes even more concerned to put into his picture all that he knows to be there. Food in the stomach is generally shown. And, by what Piaget calls 'quasi-rotation', a side view will be distorted so that both eyes, both legs and both arms are accounted for. Pamela's delicately painted picture of 'A little girl riding on a lamb' shows three instances of this quasi-rotation (the child's legs and the lamb's eyes and ears). Pamela has noticed and recorded the 'fourness'

Pamela's lamb. ('Quasi-rotation.')

of the legs and has given the 'little girl' a body. The lamb must be proportionately much more important in Pamela's thoughts than its rider.

This Picasso-like attitude, of recording faithfully all that the young artist knows really to be there, leads Piaget to call this stage of child art one of 'intellectual realism'. Julian has illustrated some of its features and Pamela others, but Pamela's picture, above all, tells us that the essence of her preconcept was of the soft woolliness of young lambs.

(c) Art in the transitional period into early school life:

For many children this stage of 'visual realism' in producing pictures will not start until they have become quite adept at intuitive thinking, but the occasional child who has had tremendous encouragement towards artistic expression may reach it before the age of five.

As the term 'visual realism' suggests, child art has now reached a stage in which the toddler begins to concentrate on reproducing all that he really sees before him. I met many children in the USSR (in something akin to English pre-school play groups) who revelled in art. So we will end here with a picture of skate-dancers painted by Shula, a Russian girl of slightly less than five years old. She painted it impulsively in a few minutes on a paper napkin that had been given to her for cleaning her

Shula's skaters. ('Visual realism.')

paintbrushes. Earlier that day she had been skating, and the picture of other skaters round her must still have been very live in her mind. She seemed to make her clear-cut brush marks with firm, almost skate-like rhythm. She was sure of what she had *seen*. It is a picture of 'visual realism', uncluttered by the blurred uncertainties of various points of view. Her rich experience of skating no longer left tangled preconcepts in her mind to confuse her thinking as she painted. Yet an impression of movement was vigorously conveyed.

Some art-lovers might look at these three developing stages of artistic expression and ask, 'Is this really progress? Is it not better to express one's thoughts and emotions in paintings than merely to record what one sees? Has it not all culminated in a state of intellectual technique overruling feelings and imaginative thoughts? Does it not show a tinge of disrespect for the emotional freedom that can be shown in the fine arts in contrast to the exactitude of visual form that photography can give? Is it like belittling Picasso when compared with Van Dyck?'

Such a critic has forgotten that we are watching progress in the total accumulation of ideas and skills that a child artist has at his disposal: we are not considering only the final skills to be achieved. We are certainly not looking only for recognition of shape. Shula, in our last example, put into her painting of the skate-dancers as much emotional enthusiasm as technical and visual skill. Her skills and her preconcepts had supported each other in their growth.

We have, of course, something else to watch for too. We are interested not only in what a child at this stage can produce in the way of artistic endeavour but also in what joy he absorbs from the whole process. Does his art widen his interest in all that he paints, opening up to him the beauty that is all around him? Through art does he attempt to share his joy with other people? In the next chapter we shall, for example, look to see how he begins to move towards appreciation of the artistic element in the rhythm and symmetry of mathematics. To finish this chapter we must turn to the more mundane matter of the child extending his interest from artistic shapes to shapes in general.

We saw Julian, when his art was only at the stage of intellectual realism, taking sufficient interest in shapes to attempt to draw them. We then followed the branch of his development along artistic lines. But not all the shapes that he copies are necessarily artistic. An alert child will copy almost anything. From that point it is not long before he is prepared to use shapes as signs and then as symbols. It will be a revelation to him, for example, to be told that a certain mixture of such symbols can 'say' his own name. If his parents respond to his demands he will gradually become absorbed in using symbols for such purposes and so will learn to write and then to read. His art will continue side by side with this process. For most of his young life he has learned to interpret the symbolization in adult gestures and in adult tones of voice and expressions of face – and ultimately in adult speech. Impulsively he has imitated them. Now, equally impulsively, he copies (and adapts to his own use) the completely abstract shapes of our writing.

WRITING ACHIEVED

The intellectual realism stage in art comes to children at varying ages according to the amount of experience they have had both in art and in all the activities that stimulate learning. Many will learn to write, therefore, before they are four years old and still more will do so before starting school at five. But parental anxieties could well hinder this process rather than hasten it. It is not necessarily wise to encourage it unless the child himself demands it. When writing results from the child's own enthusiasm it will be meaningful: writing that is achieved as a mechanical habit, motivated more by the parent than by the child, does not tie in with his preconcepts. Preconcepts are the overriding enrichment that toddlerhood needs: literacy can only be an outgrowth of them if it is to be genuine and dynamic.

To take advantage of the difference between parental encouragement and parental enforced teaching is a skill in itself, but an easily acquired one. One needs to join in with the child's spontaneous activities and interests, talking about them to build up the flow of language, before written words can have any meaning at all. When the child shows intellectual realism in his art he is poised towards taking an interest in shapes for their own sake. When he shows visual realism and when he starts to finger solid shapes and to copy them it might be a good idea to add a set of plastic letters to his hoard of toys. He may begin to copy those

James Carrington experimenting with letters.

letters or, like James Carrington, start spotting copies of their shapes elsewhere. James Carrington found them on his mother's typewriter: for a long time he was bewildered by the fact that striking a capital letter with his fingers produced a small letter on the paper above.

Derek, whom we have met several times in this book, enjoyed babyhood and toddlerhood to the full. Well before the age of three he was chattering volubly, communicating through body gestures and through painting and imitation, and obviously forming rich preconcepts. Intellectual realism was showing in his pictures early in his fourth year, and he went with his mother to buy plastic letters. When he began to find that their shapes were repeated on car number plates, on cereal packets and over shops, it was clear that he was beginning to accept mere shapes as signs. An easy way to describe what should then happen on the road towards literacy is to tell the rest of Derek's story.

Derek found other shapes to study, too, some of which were symbols and some of which were not. He fingered the repetitive designs on the wallpaper. He picked pansies and felt their shape. He drew his mother's attention to the zigzag road sign that they frequently passed and to the word 'stop' in extended letters at the road junction, to the double-arrow symbol of British Rail, and to many a symbol relating to television programmes.

Many of the empty containers that he played with had the well balanced and almost symmetrical sign 'Co-op' printed on them. There must have been something satisfying in the visual quality of that sign which registered in his mind. When the Co-op roundsman came to the door one day Derek started jumping in delight and shouting, 'Look, Mummy!' as he pointed to the badge on the roundsman's uniform. He ran and fetched a container, pointed out the symbol on it, then settled down to find several more. So far he had not associated symbols with the spoken word, but at this point his mother told him that this one showed that the man came from the 'Co-op'.

He liked his plastic letters as much as any toy and was as likely to want to take one of them for a walk as his beloved toy monkey. Gradually he formed the habit of breaking off temporarily from his other absorbing tasks to compare his plastic letters with those that he found on packages and in books, and to ask his mother if they, too, 'said' something. Those that interested him he laid out as words on the carpet, for, in the preconceptual period, a child becomes literate through whole words or phrases rather than through letters.[4] Derek soon learned to copy such words on paper in order to preserve them from the feet of the rest of the family or from the depredations of the carpet-sweeper.

He had truly caught on to the idea of literacy when this process was reversed. Suddenly there came a spate of questions. 'Mummy! What are the letters for "monkey"?' 'What are the letters for "tea-time"?' 'What are the letters for "tricycle"?' 'What are the letters for "play"?' Then came a quieter spell when he was seen to be building words for himself.

By the time Derek was four he had started writing ill-spelled statements and was struggling to read everything within his range. A few weeks later, without apparent effort and with surprising suddenness, he began to read books.

Many a parent could give a similarly enjoyable account of her own toddler's self-propelled journey toward pre-school literacy. Most would also tell of the agony of parental restraint in preventing themselves from taking the lead.

CONCLUSION

It was certainly an advantage to Derek, when he entered school at five, that he could read and write very well indeed. Many a school entrant feels a sense of security and achievement if he, too, has such success. Yet that is not to say that early literacy is at all essential. Far more essential is a full life in toddlerhood with scope for vigorous play and experiment and for frequent periods of quiet concentration whenever the child fancies it. A youngster who has had this enters school at five (or at six in most countries) with a mind full of lively preconcepts and an urge to investigate everything around him. Given these things, and a good vocabulary, he will quickly explore the literacy materials in the classroom, and writing and reading will come to him easily and rapidly.

Obviously, just as the early toddler found language an enricher of his preconcepts, the intuitive child will find that writing and reading widen his world of learning. Writing is an extension of learning through his own experiences, so it will engender more learning than reading can bring: reading is absorbing second-hand experience of the thoughts of others. He can enjoy both. He will learn from both, but more especially from analysing his own thoughts as he struggles to set them down on paper.

[4] He focuses his attention on 'gestalts' or patterns, not on details.

Even as adults we cannot learn much from reading only. Yet reading is a good way of sharing the thoughts of others and comparing them with our own. Parents and teachers who read this book will only enjoy it fully or learn fully from it if, as a consequence, they test and observe children, or unless they read it as a consequence of doing such observation and testing. Similarly they will only enjoy literature to the full if they can relate it, even to a slight extent, to an experiential life of their own.

Partial enjoyment, of course, is better than none. And like second-hand furniture or second-hand violins or paintings, the second-hand knowledge conveyed in books can be treasures beyond price or rubbish or anything in between. One can read the gems of historical research or the outpourings of the greatest poets and philosophers: equally one can read the trivial and the base. Experienced adult minds, working abstractly, can analyse and evaluate what they read: the toddler still has to take the first step along that path.

FOR THE MORE SERIOUS STUDENT
THE ROAD TO WRITING AND READING

1 The focal points in the development of pre-school art and writing are:
(a) Preconceptual development through interaction with the environment (i.e. something to want to paint or write about).
(b) Relationship with gesturing and speech.
(c) Symbolizing taking on any form available to the child (spontaneous art is one such welcome form).

2 The more advanced student will wish to be very clear about the development of *signs* and *symbols*. Piaget, throughout his works, lays great emphasis on their importance.

To recapitulate, a sign (such as the stick of the puppet in Chapter Three) signifies to the child that something greater than the sign (i.e. the puppet) is there. Such a sign can cause a child to symbolize, i.e. to create a symbol. He brings forth a symbolic action from within himself which enables him to assimilate the experience without the strain of accommodating to his problem.

Further, Piaget recognizes various classes of symbols that increase in abstractness as the intellect grows. The first category is symbols that involve only the child: Derek's chewing action (Chapter Four) was an example. Then there is symbolic play, in which a child may use one object (e.g. a daffodil) to symbolize another (the telephone). The most advanced class of symbol that a toddler might use is writing.

The written symbol must seem to him to be completely arbitrary, for he can know nothing of the historical accident and inheritance that determined our script. Consequently he can take no account of the derivations that make our written words what they are. One could, therefore, claim that written words are signs, not symbols. For, according to the previous paragraph, symbols must come from *within* the child (and not *to* him by accident). After all, one might say that Derek saw 'Co-op' as a sign. A symbol would have had to come from within Derek.

Yet we always call letters 'symbols'. How far are we justified? Does speech come from within the child? Does writing?

Piaget's explanation would be something like this. The *urge* to speak and the *urge* to write come from within the child. He learns to satisfy those urges by using the words and the letters that he has inherited. Thus he involves a spoken word to express a thought and he involves letters to symbolize that word on paper. Thus script becomes a store of adopted symbols.

Putting it another way, all a child's actions are *inter*actions with the environment. His environment has artificial as well as natural elements in it. Through interaction their essence is absorbed into him. The artificial element that he absorbs into himself includes words and letters which he can pour forth spontaneously when the urge comes. They have become part of himself.

Gestures serve two purposes: they can be expressed by one person and they can then be recognized by another. This applies to all symbols. So the symbols of writing are used for one person to convey a message and for another to receive it.

3 Symbolizing in pictures is as natural to the young toddler as it was to early cave man. At the stages of intellectual and visual realism his interest in his own paintings helps him forward in his respect for shapes. Pictures, in visual realism, take on a recognizable shapely appearance. But their borders are generally decorated by abstract designs and ripples that satisfy something of the inner self. Are these decorations his earliest writings? They are certainly symbols expressing the inner feelings that he has failed to get into his picture. They are symbols that come straight from him, and are not inherited from his predecessors.

4 So far we have stressed that the symbol must come spontaneously from within the child. We have assumed that a toddler's pictures are his own *spontaneous* response to his world. Yet in a play-group one finds a frustrating 'sameness' about many of the paintings. I see this as a sort of 'art-echolalia' (this is not a word from Piaget). Just as a toddler echoes speech from his neighbour, without taking any interest in what he is hearing and echoing, so he will copy mechanically and subconsciously his neighbour's picture, especially if an adult has praised it. Over a period of a few weeks a stereotype evolves. Stereotyping is a normal form of refuge from the movement around him that disturbs his train of thought.

5 Spontaneity in art, speech or writing can only come from a wealth of vivid ideas in the child's mind. And fluent speech is essential to fluid writing. As a child becomes accustomed to expressing his own thoughts on paper he will gradually grow towards an interest in reading the thoughts of others.

6 The 'Gestalt Theory' (or pattern-learning theory), of learning by general impact (in toddlerhood) synchronizes well with the Piagetian view of preconcepts as global and lacking in detail. But a gestalt is rigid, whereas a preconcept is mobile. Everything in the child's learning is global in this way. We shall see it again in the chapter on pre-mathematics.

CHAPTER ELEVEN

Pre-mathematical Ideas in Toddlerhood

One can imagine many a reader saying that Piaget is going a bit too far in his claim that foundations for later mathematical thought are laid in toddlerhood. Yet it is true. On reaching the end of this chapter those same readers could very well exclaim, 'I had never thought of that sort of thing as being pre-mathematics.'

So let us first look at what underlies the mathematics that most of today's adults studied in secondary school. Their mathematics may or may not have been subdivided into geometry, algebra, arithmetic and trigonometry, but they will probably agree that, before the last year or two at school, the sum total of their mathematics rested upon numbers, quantities, measurements, equalities, proportions, and shapes made up of straight and curved lines and angles. All of these demand skilled abstract thinking.

No one is claiming that your toddler is capable of the abstract thinking which is the essence of mathematics. He certainly is not. Nor is anyone claiming that he can sit down and consciously do mathematics on paper. Yet everything with which he interacts in his environment, in his life of happy, carefree play, is governed by the rhythm and symmetry of mathematical laws. For most of nature is based upon mathematical form. The child is constantly coming into contact with shapes, quantities, numbers of things. He meets simple proportions when his brother is taller than he or may eat less ice-cream. He meets measurement – a cupful of milk, enough string to tie round a particular parcel, enough kitchen-foil to cover a pie-dish. None of these things is mathematics, but each is an experience, based on material things, that illustrates pre-mathematically something that is the essence of mathematics. Each helps him towards building mathematical preconcepts that are, like all preconcepts, vague and unsteady of form and lacking in detail.

Piaget has done research into the growth of pre-mathematics in the young child in perhaps a hundred or more ways. In this short chapter there is room for only a few key examples, so let us look briefly at the growth of some preconcepts of shapes and of numbers.

We will take shapes first, for they are more easily recognized by the toddler through his senses than numbers are: we must always remember that he is still heavily dependent on his senses for his learning. Consequently he takes an enthusiastic interest in shapes and his preconcepts of shape grow quickly. All his other insubstantial preconcepts come to the aid of his senses and interweave with dawning pre-mathematical ideas. They are less substantial than the sensory experiences, so it is the learning, through his senses of sight and touch, that predominates.

I PRE-MATHEMATICAL IDEAS ABOUT SHAPES

Most parents will have seen in toyshops a wealth of specially designed play apparatus that is beautifully structured to help the toddler lay the foundations for geometrical thought. Generally such apparatus is very good. But few parents realize how many geometrical preconcepts a toddler can form, too, through play with ordinary household materials and household junk.

'Small', from Chapters Five and Six, is now just over three. His chatter seems interminable, mostly on the subject of kitchen utensils. He is as plentifully supplied with toys as most children and he has a good garden in which he and his parents play together. Their enjoyment of his company is infectious and helps to enrich his own enjoyment. So why should his attention focus on kitchenware and junk? It could well be for the social reason of his seeing adults 'play' with pots and pans too: possibly this precipitates him into imitation of adult activities and such imitation, in turn, initiates speech. The reason could equally be that the aesthetically pleasing shape of most utensils and containers activates his senses of sight and touch into appreciative response.

All Euclidean shapes are there in kitchen packages, except for the

Helen's factory.

perfect sphere. If one includes food, as well as packages, approximate spheres then appear in such items as oranges and Dutch cheese. Just look at the geometrical shapes in the factory that Helen is building from cardboard junk!

Think of the varied cylindrical shapes in a set of saucepans, in tins of scouring powder, in jam-jars and in a rolling-pin! Think of the fascinating circular shape of many a box of processed cheese with the diameters and centre clearly marked and emphasized as each section of cheese is taken out! Think of the enormous variety of rectangular surfaces of boxes and pastry-boards and garden spades! Look at the parallel rows of bunches of bristles on a rectangular nail-brush! Even the old-fashioned kitchen scrubbing-brush is symmetrical in shape and there is symmetry in the shape of a spoon, a trowel and in most of the mixing and serving gadgets that hang in a row over the kitchen stove. These are all seeds for future Euclidean geometry. Yet early pre-geometry for this youngster is much more fundamental, although less exact of course, than a study (through play) of Euclidean shapes.

A India rubber geometry

(i) What is topology?

When I was a schoolchild, topology was considered advanced mathematics. We called it 'India rubber geometry' for, in topology, Euclidean shapes can be stretched or shrunk or twisted in any direction so long as certain particular properties are preserved. Here is a list of them:
(a) No unbroken line may be broken. For example, the circumference of a circle may be stretched or twisted to a square or rectangle or triangle, or to almost any irregular shape, but it may *not* be broken to become an arc.
(b) Crossings must be retained intact and no further crossings may be made.
(c) Any feature inside another feature must remain inside. Similarly anything outside must remain outside. Such features are spoken of as 'enclosures' and 'surroundings'.
(d) Things that touch one another must continue to touch. They must neither cross nor split apart. In other words, 'continuity' must be retained and 'separations' must be respected.

Given these restrictions and liberties, the principles of 'ordinary geometry' may be carried out. Does topology seem chaotic to those of you who have never consciously studied it? Yet your eyes, refocusing as the pupils close, carry it out to some extent each time you concentrate on watching a car, with familiar people inside it, drive away along a twisting road. Your intellect copes with it to some extent whenever you see a familiar view from an entirely new angle. You cope with it completely if you see yourself in a distorting mirror. A cartoonist uses topology to stress the features of each one of his subjects.

(ii) Toddlers' topology:

Piaget has demonstrated that a young child is much more interested in the topological properties of geometry than in the Euclidean properties that comprise straight lines, regular curves and specific angles. (It may be this spontaneous interest that subtly influences the child's fondness for cartoon animals and puppets in books and on television.) Consequently, with quite a struggle, he forms early topological preconcepts: Euclidean preconcepts form at the same time, but lag behind. In two of the examples below we shall see children having difficulty with the topological problem of tying a knot and still greater difficulty in constructing a simple, Euclidean straight line.

Even a baby experiments with topological enclosure. Joanne, at eighteen months old, tried an enclosure by jamming her bricks into a toy teapot. She encircled her toys on the floor with an unusually long scarf and, with great joy, repeatedly encircled herself with a ring of plastic toys. Finding what it is like to be inside or outside gives one a feeling that is at the root of topology.

'Small', who was a year older than Joanne, studied enclosure and surroundings as he fitted small saucepans into bigger ones or as he put a potato into a saucepan and closed the lid firmly. Concurrently, and more slowly, he began to appreciate the rhythmic growth in the proportions of the perfect Euclidean circles of a set of saucepans. As he played with the long handles of forks and spoons and of the garden rake and hoe, he grew to appreciate topological crossings. The tangles he made with a hose fascinated him. Think of the pre-topology he may have enjoyed as he twisted, turned and stretched rolled-out pastry.

Children also show signs of these early topological interests in their art. If we glance back at the previous chapter we see the dawning of topological understanding as even the youngest toddler drew his mother's mouth and eyes within the outline of her face, although he failed to know whether to include or to exclude the nose. The toddler who could appreciate that his mother's limbs and body should join was topologically one stage further on, even though he had not noticed that she had a neck. So art and mathematics are very much interrelated.

Below are two of Piaget's best-known diagnostic tests of children's progress in appreciation of geometrical shapes. The first[1] is of topological properties and the second[2] is of a simple Euclidean straight line.

(iii) The topology of a simple knot:

(a) Problem 1, tying a knot. Careful scrutiny of the faces and hands of the children in the accompanying photographs should convince the reader that toddlers can feel pleasure as well as puzzlement if you present them with the problem of finding out how to tie a knot and give them only minimal help. One must emphasize 'finding out how to' as against 'being taught'. It is comparatively easy to teach quite a young toddler to perform the mechanical task of tying a knot. Our aim is to watch the struggle that goes on when he exercises his thoughts as well as his fingers in *exploring* how to tie it. He must be given the opening chance to watch an adult tie a simple knot and then no further training. It is very revealing of his pre-mathematical intellectual struggles. The experience will be of obvious value to the child too, for in toddlerhood he learns much by experimenting

Joanne. Topological enclosure.

[1] Jean Piaget and Bärbel Inhelder, *The Child's Conception of Space*, Chapter 4 and pp. 158ff.
[2] *The Child's Conception of Space*, p. 158.

Billy. Complete inability to intertwine a knot.

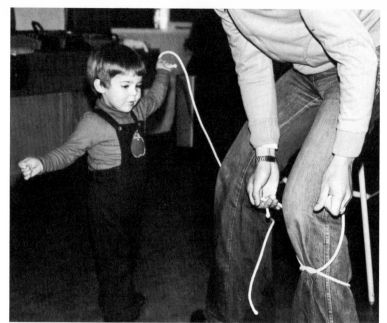

Wendy. Touching gently.

Wendy. Crossing without intertwining.

and this experiment may last him for hours. A persistent, very young toddler may perfect it only over a period of months.

For any parent who wants to try it, the experiment is quite a simple one, needing only the minimum of materials. The greatest difficulty is that of resisting the temptation to guide and teach the child.

Use several short lengths of soft cord and let your child watch you tie a loose, simple, knot in the middle of one of the lengths. Encourage him to pull it tight to make sure that it *is* a knot and then loosen it again. As he loosens it you may point out to him the under-over sequence very briefly (i.e. avoid any training element), and you will find that if he is nearing four or more he will become very interested. Nevertheless, he will find it extremely difficult to hold the pattern in his head if you then ask him to tie one just like it. Leave yours lying beside him as he tries: he may finger it if he wishes.

The following photographs illustrate the typical reactions that Piaget picked out as the hallmarks of the stages of development in a child's thinking about this problem. The child is trying to cope with three puzzles at one time (shape, crossing and intertwining) and each is a challenge to him.

Billy, at a little less than four, enjoyed the game of trying to copy a knot tied round a student's leg, but had no success. Nor could he do other than hope for the cord to take form when he tried to tie it over the arm of a chair. He did not even cross the cord at all, although he tried with enthusiasm for more than a quarter of an hour.

In order to make the problem seem more like a game the following three children had been given a 'spaceman's belt', complete with flashing light, to tie round the waist by cords at each end.

Wendy, at four years and a month old, watched a specimen knot tied and laid beside her around a jar. She seemed not to notice the intertwining. At first she only brought the ends of her own cord together to touch one another, as if she expected that by some magic they might fuse. When she had failed several times in such attempts she tried a simple pulling across. Her movements suggested that a further demonstration had alerted her to noticing that crossing was involved. She persisted in this, crossing left over right and then right over left, time after time. After yet another demonstration (probably more than should have been given) she grew even more confident than before that the cord must cross, so she tried several crossings in one effort. Unfortunately some of them cancelled out others and once more she was left with a singly crossed cord. She persisted at intervals for an hour or so, but had no greater success.

Anthony, four months older than Wendy, had what he considered immediate success. He wound the cord several times round itself, putting so much strength into it that the cord held for a few minutes. Each time it fell apart he wound it again, even more tightly. He was quite sure that he had tied a knot.

Martyn was a month or two older still. He concentrated for a very long time. At each attempt he managed to make a loop and to pass an end through it. Then he stopped to examine it before dropping the loop and starting again. He had been at hand to watch Anthony's efforts and seemed to have learned that further twisting would not secure the 'knot', but, try as he might, he could find no way of securing its passage through that one loop.

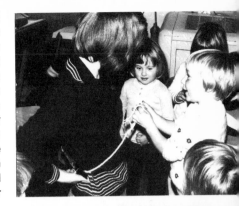

Anthony trusting to strength.

These are typical of the results that we find with almost every child in the preconceptual period of childhood. The youngest always try touching the ends gently together in simple trust. The next stage is always either crossing or looping. Very rarely can the children carry in their minds the possibility of experimenting with both crossing and looping jointly for one purpose. All the children photographed above were at nursery school, but a few others of more than four and a half, in their own homes, did with great effort succeed in tying a knot. They were able to have much longer unhindered periods of struggling with it.

Such experiments[3] leave one in no doubt of the intense interest in the pre-geometry of crossing and enclosing that young children can sustain. In general it can be said that the ability to puzzle out the whole complicated problem, without coaching or drilling, matures at between about four and about five years of age.

As soon as a child can *tie* a knot Piaget brings in a further challenge, to test whether the child does or does not *appreciate* the intertwining of the knot that he can tie.

Martyn almost achieves interlinking.

[3] It is worth noticing in passing that the above was also an example of parallel play. No child except Martyn *chose* to attempt to tie the knot on anyone except an adult. Even in his case Martyn held no conversation whatsoever (not even an initial request) with Sally, and she, as his dummy, was relaxed and unconcerned. None showed any interest in anything except the knot and the students: the knot held intense interest and the students inspired a little spontaneous conversation. Yet, at a glance it would have seemed that all were playing socially.

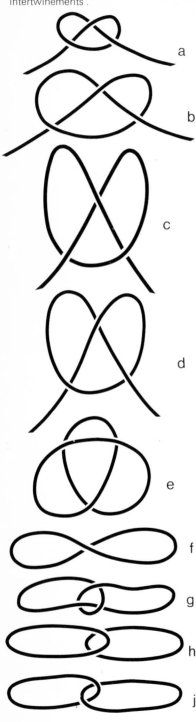

Piaget's knots and 'false intertwinements'.

a

b

c

d

e

f

g

h

j

(b) Problem 2, recognition of true knots: To carry out this further probe parents will need more pieces of soft cord, some of which are stuck or spliced into rings, others into interlocking rings and still others that are shaped into loose knots. All can be seen in the diagrams. The diagrams show, too, some lengths of string that are merely cross-overs, giving what Piaget calls 'false knots' or 'false interlinkings'. It would be wise also to have spare cord available in case the child wants to experiment with the shapes for himself.

The child is allowed to follow round each specimen with his fingers, but otherwise not to touch it, as he is asked the following questions. With all examples one must probe into the reasons for his answers, for it is the child's *thoughts* that we are examining. Otherwise answers could be a mere gamble. One must also be quite sure that the child understands each question. As in the case of all Piagetian tests, one needs to know the child's full thinking on the problem and to get some idea of how genuine his interest is in trying to solve it.

Question 1: Would *a* and *b* tighten into knots if one pulled the ends of the string? Then ask similarly about *c* and *d*.

Question 2: Could *a* and *b* be made into the same-shaped knot as each other without first being untied?

Question 3: Apply question 2 to *c* and *d* and then to *b* and *d*.

Question 4: Could *e* be opened into a ring? Ask the same about *f* and *g*.

Question 5: Could *h* and then *j* be pulled apart?

Nicola had proved herself able to tie a simple knot. She was the youngest child tested by my team to have any success with these five questions.

Nicola could see the similarity between *a* and *b* but she also hesitantly considered *c* and *d* to be identical. She could not even consider that *b* and *d* had any similarity to one another. She was confident that *f* would open into a ring but she was too confused to make up her mind about *e*. She was sure that *g* could not be opened, but was equally sure that both *h* and *j* could be pulled apart. When we laid before her a false simple knot she considered it was 'a knot that would tie tightly, but not like the others'.

As we analyse this we must come to the conclusion that, although Nicola had learned through constant trial and error how to tie knots, the pattern of intertwining could not be held steadily in her mind. It was still preconceptual. Identical knots such as *a* and *b* could be seen to be identical while they were laid in similar shape, but when one was given the shape of wings, as in *d*, the impact on her senses overpowered her thinking and she could no longer consider the similar topology of two visually dissimilar shapes. Neither could she concentrate on the direction of intertwining. In fact, she could not handle intertwining *in her mind* at all as her response to the false knot showed. She could suspect a difference between *c* and *d* but could not identify it.

This confusion between trusting to sight and trusting to one's insecure preconceptual knowledge is typical of the transitional stage that Piaget found in many children. It is, of course, also a general characteristic of preconceptual intellect as well as of the intuitive decision-making that emerges at this age. It took an eight-year-old to answer correctly these and some more complicated questions about knots laid before her. A girl

Nicola partly able to intertwine in her mind.

of the age of Caroline, of course, gave the right answers, but only after long and serious consideration.

(c) Why? 'Why all this trouble about knots', you might ask, 'when it is fairly easy to teach my child to tie them?'

One answer is that a study of the three-dimensional course the string takes as a knot is tied poses problems for the child about the course of a point moving through space. It is probable that a child lays pre-geometrical foundations by struggling with such problems, and these struggles start off paths of learning for later days. The final chapter of this book, on memory and intelligence, will enlarge on this theme but not on this particular example of it.

There is a second answer to the question. It could teach us, as adults, that a toddler or infant makes his decisions more from an impact glance at the general pattern[4] than through analysing structures thoughtfully. It helps us to see that, in topological matters (in this case crossings and enclosures), his thinking remains preconceptual well into infancy. It should warn us to be patient when a task that he has before him demands topological thought. He needs the time to learn to think very slowly, without distraction. So long as he is concentrating it is better that he should go on puzzling, unhindered by any child or by an impatient adult. One does not 'help' by training him to a technique, or by doing a job for him, at the cost of disturbing the early growth of thinking patterns that are to be the mainstay of his educational life. He can learn more by experience than by persuasion. Early education is not just a culling of facts: it is a learning how to learn.

Caroline mentally appreciates intertwinement.

[4] This substantiates the Gestalt Theory of psychology and so the modern way of teaching reading by recognition of whole words or whole phrases.

James Carrington handles straight and
curved railway track.

James Carrington appreciates
straightness.

B Euclidean pre-geometry

Problems with straight lines:

The average young toddler has plenty of experience with lines. Many of
these lines are more or less straight, but he seems peculiarly oblivious of
the fact. The word 'line' becomes meaningful to him through
conversation as he helps his mother to hang linen on a line, through her
drawing his attention to traffic lines painted on the road and through his
father's line of sticks in the vegetable garden. He has probably leaned
down and fingered enquiringly the lines of cracks between paving-stones
and he knows that when he scribbles on paper the resulting marks are
called 'lines'. So he has an insubstantial preconcept of lines.

There are other lines that he is subconsciously aware of, although
adults rarely call them lines. For instance, there is the line demarcating the
edge of the hearthrug on the carpet along which his father may have set
out a line of soldiers in play.

We have seen that a young toddler is not as easily interested in whether
lines are straight or curved, or whether objects are square, as he is in
stretchings and crossings and twistings and inclusions. But, by the
middle of toddlerhood, he becomes able to perceive that a line is straight
and intuitively to respond to straightness. Yet he cannot recognize
straightness as such, holding it in his mind to carry out a task. Intuitively
he lets the splashed blobs of his paintings give way to straight-lined
outlines of houses, but the sheer abstraction of straightness is beyond his
understanding.

Piaget devised a very simple game to diagnose[5] the development of a
child's thinking about straightness and we carried it out with James

[5] Jean Piaget and Bärbel Inhelder, *The Child's Conception of Space*, pp. 156ff.

Carrington. To play the game enjoyably one needs a rectangular-topped table (to represent a field) and about a dozen or so matchsticks, each stuck into a blob of plasticine (to represent telegraph poles that have to be erected across the field in a straight line, not parallel to the sides). With James we used small counters that he was playing with, on an inverted box that had held his railway track.

One must first make sure that the child can *perceive* straightness. James had been sorting out straight from curved sections of railway track and using the words repeatedly. He had pulled a skipping-rope with his grandfather and made sure that it was straight. But we took the essential precaution of *not* drawing his attention to the straight sides of the box, for we wanted to test whether his sensual perception of them would overrule his preconcept of straightness in the line that he was trying to construct. We laid down the first and last counters (these can be seen clearly in the photograph, near the bottom left and top right corners of the box) and asked James Carrington if he could place the others 'to make a beautifully straight line all the way between them'. I even flicked my hand across in the diagonal line.

James took over with delight. The result was an almost zigzag line running at times parallel with the bottom straight edge of the box and at other times parallel with the side. All along its course it seemed to be influenced by the side nearest to it: in the middle it became wavy. James was proud of it and was sure that it was straight. That evening, spontaneously, he took to finger-painting and painted for me a picture of straight lines: it is autographed in the top left corner, but the reader may have to hunt for the five letters of the name. A finely ruled rectangle has been added to help the reader locate James's signature.

James Carrington's crooked 'straight line'.

James Carrington's evocation of straight lines.

Basil checking for Euclidean straightness.

James Carrington's 'straight' line of counters was quite an achievement for his age. This was partly because he spends so much of his time playing with toys (structured toys and junk) that have mathematical values. He chatters incessantly about them with his parents and the rest of the family. But one can see that in spite of this his line was more influenced by intuitive reference to the sides of the box than related to the straight line that he was trying to hold in his mind. Piaget found that children at not quite such an advanced stage as James produced right-angled results, parallel first with one side and then with the other. When the test was set on a circular table the line was dragged into a curve.

An older child, who has had equally rich experience with toys and with adult involvement, may have formed a very strong preconcept or even a concept of straightness by the age of about five. Basil, at five years and a month, illustrated this for us in the normal course of his building a brick garage for his cars: he sprawled down and took a line of sight. Euclid could hardly have asked for more to illustrate one of his definitions of a straight line as one progressing continuously in the same direction.[6] It will be seen that Basil ignored the help that the carpet edge could have given him; he knew the line that he wanted.

II PRE-MATHEMATICAL IDEAS OF NUMBER

Your child in his pre-school period will begin to get a fairly strong feeling of number if you employ his help in number-tasks about the house, counting as you go. But the cautious parent will remember that any number is a complete abstraction, imperceptible to any of the senses. For example, the number five is not the cipher 5, nor the word, nor is it an adjective pinpointing five cups and saucers as the word 'blue' might be. It is an abstract collectiveness common to any group of five things. Many an adult cannot think clearly about abstracts. Certainly a pre-school child cannot. Yet even such a small child can form habits of dealing physically with small numbers so that gradually he forms preconcepts about them.

Take the example of 'three blue plates'. He can see and feel plates. He can see blue. He cannot experience 'three' with any of his senses; he can only sense something of the idea of 'enough for Mummy and Daddy and me'. 'Three red strawberries' can denote the same threeness, but only the redness and the strawberries can affect his senses of taste, sight, touch and smell. He can see *that there are* three but he cannot *see* three. The actual threeness is an abstraction.

Let us take two true stories.

Briony, aged five, was walking with her father when they met a woman with five lively dachshund puppies on a multiple lead. Briony squealed with delight as her father asked, 'How many are there?' 'One, two, three, four, five, six, seven!' recited Briony. 'Seven, I counted them.' She did not, in fact count. She only recited.

Derek, when he was so young that he had to stand on tiptoes to get his chin on the table, was in his kitchen with both parents, two sisters and

---

[6] Euclid's other definition is 'the shortest distance between two points'.

two visiting children when I entered. Seven bowls and spoons were on the table and his mother was at the draining-board cutting up a brick of ice-cream. Derek became anxious. He went repeatedly to the table and peered at the bowls (or at one bowl at a time; one could not tell). Each time he scrutinized one person. Then he went to his mother and said, 'Mummy, there are not enough bowls now Mary Sime has come.'

Which child, Briony or Derek, was further on the path towards a concept of number? Briony could recite numbers but could not count. Derek could neither count nor recite numbers, but he had a sense of 'enoughness' that could be the seed of an imminent preconcept of number.

Now for a third story:

By chance I met a mother and her toddler in the village street. The child was hopping energetically between occasional landmarks, counting as he hopped. 'One, two, three, four, five,' he panted as he hopped from a jutting-out doorstep to a dustbin for sale outside a hardware shop. His mother was counting quietly with him. She added gently, 'Five hops! Good! You just did it, didn't you?' And they went on walking quietly together, I presume until the next convenient landmark.

What better example could one have of learning number through experience?

If, in a few weeks time, his mother wants to diagnose his concept or preconcept of number, she could well start with the test we gave to Hannah that is recorded on page 76.

CONCLUSION

Any concerned parents can do wonders in educating their own children in pre-mathematics, as in most subjects, both before schooling and during school life, and can trust that no harm will be done so long as they are taught through experience and not predominantly through talk and/or drilling. In teaching the child number there is the one real danger of being tempted to forget the story of Briony and merely teaching him, uselessly, to recite number words. One can, however, always avoid possible dangers by taking two precautionary steps. One must first examine, in one's own thinking, the absolute essence of the concept one is trying to help him form. Then one can probe the stage of his thinking by using the appropriate Piagetian test or observation. When you know what his relevant convictions really are you can then supply him with the further enriching experiences that are, to him, work that is as enjoyable as play.

If a child enters school at five or six with fairly strong preconcepts and meets a teacher whose own mathematics is sound, then he should, within about two years, strengthen his preconcepts into full concepts which will become tools for all future reasoned learning. Never hesitate to continue to help him pragmatically rather than with mere words. Pragmatic help from parents will always be real help, however poor or however good his teaching at school might be. Given such help in the early stages, absolutely free of drilling, every child of average ability can grow to find enormous pleasure later in life in the richness of mathematical exploration. Mathematics is not just a 'useful subject'. It has a beauty and elegance[7] that all too few of us enjoy. It is an elegance similar to that of poetry or of good music. There is the subtle difference that such elegance can be enjoyed in poetry and in music throughout life but the elegance in mathematics is only revealed by the abstract thinking that comes in adolescence: your child needs the pragmatic foundation-laying that must stretch through all primary school life before the true richness of mathematics can reach him.

FOR THE MORE SERIOUS STUDENT
MATHEMATICAL PRECONCEPTS

Most of the points made in this chapter do not need elaboration. A great many themes essential to mathematical thinking could not be touched upon in the space of this book. The most essential are mentioned on pages 119–29.

The serious student should also read more about the concept of numbers, cardinal and ordinal, in Piaget's *The Child's Conception of Number*. Various technical terms will appear (e.g. 'one-to-one correspondence') but all are fairly obvious in meaning.

It is equally important to read *The Early Growth of Logic in the Child*, as logic is so entangled with mathematics that neither can grow healthily without the other. Preconcepts that are the forerunners of logic are nurtured throughout toddlerhood in abundant experiential play.

Mathematics, like language, is one of the five cornerstones of all later learning. Not only is it enjoyable in its own right, but its patterns and skills influence all learning, both in other subjects of the school curriculum and in life as a whole. The ideal breeding ground for it is in the child's own home in pre-school days.

[7] I owe the word 'elegance' to Professor Paul Black. It strikes me as a perfect word for the purpose.

CHAPTER TWELVE

The 'Black Box' of Memory

Piaget's recently translated *Memory and Intelligence* is as exciting in its theme as almost any of his previous works. At the risk of over-simplification, his theme could be said to be as follows.

Small children who enjoy meaningful experiences subconsciously select from those experiences the most crucial factors. They not only catalogue these factors into a memory storehouse but also absorb selected vivid elements of any experience into what Piaget calls the 'black box' of memory. The 'black box' is a subconscious laboratory of the mind in which such items, instead of lying dormant until recalled, are kept fully active. The subconscious activity restructures each experience so that it may be recalled (perhaps years later) not in its original form but enriched, to keep pace with the child's general growth of intellectual patterns and skills across that time. In consequence, when some incident triggers the emergence of memories of the original experience, they come forth re-formed as apparent memories of far more than did, in fact, happen at the time. The child who tells of them can seem to be lying while he is, on the contrary, completely convinced that he is reporting the truth.

This claim is in strong contrast to the theories of most earlier psychologists who saw memory as an absolute, non-selective recording of the whole of any experience, and considered all acts of recall to be direct reconstructions of the information that went in. The Freudian school certainly believed that unconscious memories could activate neurotic illnesses: that is very different from saying that memories could solve their own problems and so could, themselves, emerge transformed.

Piaget gives plentiful examples of this subconscious growth of specific memories as they can be monitored in children right up to mid-adolescence. The activity in the 'black box' would seem to be *inter*action, not just action. It would seem that the intellect uses items of memory as the raw materials of subconscious experimentation. The experimentation enables the intellect to mature: correspondingly the subconsciously maturing intellect has its impact on its raw materials (the particular memories), causing them to grow too.

LIFE IN THE 'BLACK BOX'

Piaget set out to explore the 'black box' by giving children, from early toddlerhood onwards, enjoyable problems to solve. Many of those problems were closely related to the ones recorded in his previous books. Once each child had pondered his problem for a reasonable amount of time Piaget, and those around him, removed the apparatus and carefully refrained from referring to the experience again for selected periods. The periods varied from a week to six weeks or six months to a year. Children who had solved the problem dropped out of the experiment completely.

At the end of the period of dormancy the experimenters used some slight reminder to trigger the child into recalling the experience. Clinical care was taken that the reminder should not be of such a nature as to jog his memory by any hint or by any leading question that could remind the child of the essence of the problem.

The staggering result was that in the vast majority of cases children's memories tended to deteriorate in the shorter period: yet they seemed to have grown over the longer periods to the extent that the children 'recalled' having solved problems which they did not, at the time, actually solve. This was not just wishful thinking, because they could explain the solution that they felt sure they had given in spite of the fact that really they had found none at the time. They did not even need the adult to tell them what the problem had been.

In each specific case, when the testing had been completed and the enhanced memory recorded, the child was given further conventional tests to ascertain what his general intellectual development had been over the same interval of time. In all recorded cases the two developments were found to synchronize.

As in the case of all Piagetian tests, probing was carried out to make sure of the child's full thinking on the matter: no impulsively hazarded answers were accepted at face value.

HOW COULD THIS HAPPEN?

This state of affairs can only be accounted for by activity in the 'black box' of the memory.

We can all accept that during the intervening period each child will have developed intellectually. He will possibly even have moved into a later major period (or sub-period) of intellectual growth. We expect this intellectual growth to influence his conscious or subconscious solving of new problems, or even of problems brought before him for a second time. What Piaget now reveals is different: it is that, in the storehouse of memory, the child's maturing intellect has been actively metamorphosing memories that were stacked there and making them satisfy his new, advanced way of thinking. The child, during the process, was unconscious of it all. So when a memory of a year ago is recalled it can come forth today as if it had in the first instance been understood with today's intellect. Within the 'black box', memory is constantly restructuring and reorganizing all that it selects as being of major interest

Anna's memory of an experience.

and value. Memories and growing mental skills interlink to give maximum growth advantage, one to the other.

This can be illustrated by the short story of Anna.

In the February before she entered school, and about a year before the accompanying photograph was taken, Anna was allowed to play with the materials for a Piagetian prelogic test. It was a double clothes-line with an odd number of garments clipped to the top line and an abundant supply of further garments for her to play with. Its purpose is to test a child's concept of sequence.

On the first occasion it had been put before Anna merely to keep her contented so that she should not disturb her brother. Nevertheless Anna asked to be 'played with too' so, before taking it from her, I had asked her the test question, 'Could you find the right clothes to hang on the bottom line to make it exactly like my line at the top?'

Anna had been delighted to comply. With encouragement she had found the right garment to start the new line, but then exuberance led her to continue to hang every available garment on one line or the other. This was all repeated two or three times before I picked up the lines and took them right away. Anna had spasmodically tried to do as she was asked but her real interest at the time, and with her parents that evening, had been focused on the fun of hanging up laundry and of being photographed. Her parents feel sure that from that day onwards Anna never mentioned the line again and in her village school neither of the two teachers had any idea of the existence of such a line (or of its purpose).

Just over a year later Anna and I met by chance. She ran to me and greeted me with the news, 'Marysime! Nicolas has his picture in a book.' She did not seem to remember that I had taken his picture. I asked her if she had had her picture taken at the same time and she replied, with a touch of jealousy in her voice, 'Yes! And I was hanging washing but Nicky was only drawing funny shapes.' 'Tell me more!' I said, 'Where were you hanging washing?'

Enthusiastically Anna drew her hand along in a horizontal line high in the air, saying, 'There were dresses and things on that top line and I had to put some just like them on the bottom line like this.' She flicked both her hands down half a dozen times from the top line to an equally imaginary bottom line in quick, parallel, vertical strokes.

Obviously she was remembering more of her experience and of the problem than she had comprehended at the time. I remarked that I had a line like that and took her, with her father willingly in tow, to a workroom where all the necessary materials were available. She chattered volubly all the way, so it was easy for me not to refer to the problem in hand until I had confronted her with the double lines and hung a top row of five garments.

'That's right!' said Anna. 'That's what it was like.'

Without waiting for me to finish she had started selecting the first garment, talking all the time and explaining that she was looking for 'a blouse like that top one'. Then she struggled on, unaided in any way, until the bottom line was hung accurately. She had to give it a lot of thought, all of which she expressed aloud, for she was a talkative child. Her running commentary was so convincing that there was little need to probe for her full thinking. At the end I praised her line and simply asked, 'Did you do it exactly like that before?' 'Yes!' said Anna with pride and then, with minimal pause, 'When will *those* photos be done?'

So Anna's 'black box' had, at least during some part of the year, been a hive of industry rather than a deserted store room. It is a clear example of Piaget's claim that, as a child's periods of intellectual growth progress his apparent memories can also grow out of all recognition to correspond with the increase in intellectual growth. Further diagnostic tests revealed that, during the year, Anna had progressed from the preconceptual to the intuitive period of thinking. In other words Anna's 'black box' had been a busy workroom, servicing at least this one memory to keep it up to date.

Anna's example also emphasizes the fact that Piagetian diagnosis can often be carried out by observation as well as by deliberate testing if one knows the essence of his theories well. Nevertheless it is wise to use his tests as frequently as one wishes for they are as enjoyable to the child as any form of play and they are subtly so devised as to reveal the child's thinking with clarity and certainty.

CONCLUSION

It is not only in toddlers that 'black box' activity goes on. Memory is alive and active in all of us, however much we bury it in our subconscious in order to dwell consciously on enjoying the pleasures and solving the problems that face us day by day. Certainly adults who take interest in these theories have all reached the period of hypothetical thinking and abstract reasoning. Yet our mental skills still go on increasing as years full of experiences go by: theoretically they increase as the experiences of each day affect us. We must have seething activity in our 'black boxes' too, although generally we are unconscious of the fact. Occasionally we realize that, unaccountably, we have solved a problem that we had abandoned, but such a pleasant experience is all too rare.

FOR THE MORE SERIOUS STUDENT

Memory and Intelligence is very simply written in twenty short chapters and is, perhaps, the easiest of all Piaget's books to read. Each chapter takes one specific example of the 'black box' servicing a memory. Each is applicable to children of a specific age. Because it is such easy reading no further examples will be given here. Any student who has read this book so far should find reward in reading at least a few chapters of *Memory and Intelligence* in Piaget's original (of course, translated) words.

Such a student might then compare and contrast his findings with the thinking of other major psychologists.

It is particularly worth contrasting them with the 'non-selective' theories of Freud and Bergson who saw the role of memory as conserving the whole past in such a way that it is organized directly and determined to the last detail by circumstances and by the very passage of time. Similarly William James (and others) believe all acts of recall to be direct reconstruction of the original experience.

The crucial point of contrast is that for Piaget the very dynamism of the child (or adult), as he interacts with his environment, determines both his intellectual growth and his memory. It is also interesting to compare *Memory and Intelligence* with the results shown by current research into intellectual development during sleep (known to most casual readers as 'rapid eye movement research'), which could well substantiate Piaget's findings.

CODA

With Anna's simple but rich example to illustrate the dynamism of memory, we round off this brief summary of most of the mainstreams of intellectual growth in the child from birth until the age of about five.

Many more chapters could have been written. It would have been interesting to examine in detail the peculiar convictions that the very young can hold and that we might never suspect. Here are some random examples:

Derek, whom we recorded splashing through a pool in Chapter Seven, thought that his name was made inside him and could not be changed.

David, from the introduction to Section II ('train go in dark'), watched me put my car in the garage and said, in gentle tones, 'Give it a drink of petrol and put it to bed.'

Another toddler asked, 'Does the wind like blowing my pages over?'

Yet another tried to prevent her father covering the car windscreen with newspaper, anchored by the windscreen-wipers, to prevent ice forming on a frosty night. 'Don't Daddy!' she pleaded. 'It won't be able to see.'

Claire Denyse and Sam, like most children of about two, are seen here fascinated by a rabbit. They are not quite sure how to sort out live things from the inanimate. After all, the autumn leaves are moving about more (in the wind) than the rabbit is doing!

Susan, mentioned in the companion book, had sat beside her mother throughout several television newsreels one day, watching, enthralled, as the first men landed on the moon. As her mother undressed her that night, with the moon gleaming through the window, she asked Susan how big she thought the moon was. Susan gestured the size with her hands. Her replies to further questions made it quite clear that she was sure it could be no bigger. Then her mother said, 'But you have just been watching men walk on it! Haven't you?' To which Susan merely shrugged her shoulders and responded, 'Oh! That moon!' Yet the same Susan was equally sure that the frog they had found near a pond several miles from the house was the same frog that they had in their own garden: she seemed to take it for granted that there was only one frog in the world, for she had never seen more than one at a time.

Claire Denyse and Sam. What is life?

THE QUESTION 'WHY . . . ?'

These peculiar convictions, like the acceptance of magic, are held within what might almost be seen as a safety-valve which prevents the mind from becoming over-anxious about happenings that the youngster cannot manipulate or understand. Often this is because he cannot appreciate the equilibrium between cause and effect.

Certainly we have recorded, even in early babyhood, a child trying to study cause and effect from direct experience (keeping the toy swinging in the baby-carriage roof). Yet we have seen that a much older child cannot consider cause and effect in matters that he cannot himself control and that he cannot experience through his senses. Derek is just beginning seriously to study cause and effect as he shoots marbles down a ramp that can be tilted at varied angles.

Derek. What is force?

At an early age the child grows to accept the sequences within routines. For him such sequences are the same thing as cause and effect. Anything else just receives from him bland acceptance. This even shows in his language. He rarely uses the word 'because' correctly. Shoals of his questions begin with 'What . . . ?' or 'Where . . . ?' or 'When . . . ?', but any 'Why . . . ?' questions, such as 'Why must I go to bed yet?', are rhetorical with no desire for an answer. He wants only to delay going to bed.

THE EARLY GROWTH OF LOGICAL REASONING

All these examples make one realize that the most enthralling of the further themes that might have gone into this book is that of creativity of thought and the early growth of logical reasoning. It has hardly been touched on so far, except indirectly through a few examples of illogicality. Yet, although the world 'logic' has hardly been mentioned, the reader who thinks back will realize that all toddlers' activities which have been examined have shown (obliquely) a very gradual movement towards logical expression. Toddlerhood is a period of illogical thinking: we have stressed all along that preconcepts are conglomerate rather than orderly. It is in the very process of trying to untangle his preconcepts, however unsuccessfully, that the toddler lays foundations for logical skills.

The reader may, therefore, wonder all the more why we have no chapter here on logical and creative thought. One reason is that it might have seemed less appropriate here than in the companion volume, which stresses intellectual growth during schooldays and student life. It is more important in that volume because, although its seeds and seedlings can be seen dimly in preconceptual years, its rapid growth begins only after about the age of five.

An understanding of the initial moves towards logical thinking is essential to an examination of its further growth. In *A Child's Eye View*, therefore, we look at early logic first of all through the eyes of a pre-school child struggling to sort out the disorder of his illogical thoughts. Then we continue to monitor the growth of his logical thinking right through to the beginning of adult life. We watch as the young person gradually becomes able to reason out cause and effect, then is able to foresee possibilities, to postulate probabilities and to set out to prove or disprove them. It is not all scientific. Ultimately he will be able to imagine the fantastic and the impossible and to manipulate them in far-fetched literature or in science fiction. He will represent them in art and music and in movement. And he will distinguish the true from the false.

Mathematical development is treated in *A Child's Eye View* in a rather similar way. We look back into toddlerhood at some mathematical preconcepts, such as number, and at others not referred to in this book (particularly spatial ones); then we follow their growth through infancy and through later school life.

In this way we watch preconcepts mature into simple full concepts in a variety of fields.

Most simple concepts mature during infancy. There are some simple concepts that mature later, such as the concepts of weight and time. And there are secondary concepts (for example, of proportion or of equity) that mature only when abstract thinking is possible. It is fascinating to watch them all emerge and grow.

CONCLUSION

Intellectual growth is an ever-maturing process with new techniques emerging and developing all the time. These new techniques add to and substantiate the first learning processes. They need never wear out nor be wasted. They carry the average person through the five clearly recognizable major periods of his intellectual life. There are no sharp dividing lines between these periods, as *A Child's Eye View* shows. We have seen babyhood merge into toddlerhood. Toddlerhood merges into the intuitive life of the five- and six-year-old; intuition and conceptualization gradually give way to the junior's ragged reasoning; as junior days reach their climax a very gradual movement starts towards the abstract creative thoughts of late adolescence and adulthood.

A skilled teacher needs to gear his or her styles of teaching to fit in with the different sorts of receptiveness in the brain at each age. By studying children's developmental psychology a wise teacher can plan how to encourage and help each new technique of learning in each child's repertoire, and add speed and efficiency to his whole learning process.

And the parent can always help at all ages. The foundations are best laid during babyhood and toddlerhood in the happy serenity of the home. Lack of serenity can crack such foundations and perhaps result, much later, in tumultuous thought and behaviour. Firm foundations never fail.

It is probably in toddlerhood that such healthy learning becomes most apparent to the observant parent. Yet the toddler's continuous expenditure of abundant energy in play can blind parents to his intellectual growth. It can make toddlerhood seem to be a period of physical growth only. Physical movement and mental growth are essential partners: neither can grow to the full without the other. In his very exuberance at overcoming a play problem, such as pulling a stick through a gate, every baby learns abundantly if he is given a chance to concentrate in the moments that he needs to do so.

It is a wise parent who can generally refrain from interrupting him (and who will not allow others to do so) when he is absorbed in such thought, who can learn how and when to suggest new lines of thought and investigation into his environment, who can bring her conversation to his level without being condescending about it.

A wise parent or teacher knows, too, when to interrupt him so as to train him gently but firmly to self-discipline and to respect the thoughts and needs of others in his environment. Self-discipline is a concept as dynamic as any other. So both patience and guidance are needed. The child cannot begin the logical sorting-out of his own thoughts when he has turmoil and distractions around him. If he is generally confident he can, however, accept wisely given correction.

All these well laid foundations ensure the growth of an intelligent, confident and characterful personality in a child, and he can be expected to grow up to enjoy life to the full and to contribute constructively and peacefully to the community in which he will live.

BIBLIOGRAPHY

Books by Jean Piaget

published by Routledge & Kegan Paul Ltd, London:

The Child's Conception of Number (with A. Szeminska), 1952 (U.S. Humanities Press Inc.).

The Child's Conception of Physical Causality, 1930 (U.S. Humanities Press Inc.).

The Child's Conception of Time, 1970 (U.S. Basic Books Inc.).

The Child's Conception of Movement and Speed, 1970 (U.S. Humanities Press Inc.).

The Child's Conception of the World, 1929 (U.S. Humanities Press Inc.).

The Child's Construction of Reality, 1955 (U.S. and Canada: Basic Books Inc.).

Insights and Illusions of Philosophy, 1972 (U.S. and Canada: World Publishing Co.).

Judgement and Reasoning in the Child, 1928 (U.S. Humanities Press Inc.).

The Language and Thought of the Child, 1926 (U.S. Humanities Press Inc.).

The Mechanisms of Perception, 1969 (U.S. Basic Books Inc.).

Memory and Intelligence, 1973 (U.S. Basic Books Inc.).

The Moral Judgement of the Child, 1932 (U.S. Free Press).

The Origin of Intelligence in the Child, 1953 (U.S. International Universities Press).

Play, Dreams and Imitation in Childhood, 1951 (U.S. W.W. Norton & Co. Inc.).

The Principles of Genetic Epistemology, 1972 (U.S. Basic Books Inc.).

The Psychology of Intelligence, 1950 (U.S. Routledge & Kegan Paul).

Structuralism, 1971 (U.S. Basic Books Inc.).

With Bärbel Inhelder
The Child's Conception of Geometry (with A. Szeminska), 1960 (U.S. Basic Books Inc.).

The Child's Conception of Space, 1956 (U.S. Humanities Press Inc.).

The Early Growth of Logic in the Child: Classification and Seriation, 1964 (U.S. Harper & Row).

The Growth of Logical Thinking From Childhood to Adolescence, 1958 (U.S. and Canada: Basic Books Inc.).

Mental Imagery in the Child, 1970 (U.S. Basic Books Inc.).

The Psychology of the Child, 1969 (U.S. and Canada: Basic Books Inc.).

With Paul Fraisse
Experimental Psychology: Its Scope and Method (9 vols.), vol. 1 (1968), vol. 4 (1970), vol. 5 (1968), vol. 7 (1969) (U.S. Basic Books Inc.).

published by Hodder and Stoughton Ltd, London:

Six Psychological Studies, 1969

Books by A.A. Milne

published by Methuen Children's Books, Associated Book Publishers Ltd, London

The House at Pooh Corner, 1928 (U.S. E.P. Dutton and Co. Inc.).

When We Were Very Young, 1924 (U.S. E.P. Dutton and Co. Inc.).

By Noam Chomsky

published by Temple Smith Ltd, London:
Reflections on Language, 1976

INDEX

Index of most important references only. Many key words (e.g. assimilation) will be found in numerous other places in the book.